IS THE
WHOLE BODY
A TONGUE?

IS THE WHOLE BODY A TONGUE?

edited by
Don W. Hillis

BAKER BOOK HOUSE
Grand Rapids, Michigan

Printed in the United States of America

CONTENTS

INTRODUCTION—TONGUES: UPDATING
SOME OLD ISSUES 7
  Eternity editorial

1. THE NEW CHARISMATICS...................11
  James W. L. Hills

2. FACING THE ISSUE OF TONGUES 21
  Stanley Gundry

3. THE USE AND ABUSE OF TONGUES (Part 1) 31
  Theodore Epp and John I. Paton

4. THE USE AND ABUSE OF TONGUES (Part 2) 45
  Theodore Epp and John I. Paton

5. SPEAKING IN TONGUES (Part 1) 53
  Richard W. De Haan

6. SPEAKING IN TONGUES (Part 2) 67
  Richard W. De Haan

7. IS THE CHARISMATIC MOVEMENT OF GOD? 79
  Dick Meier

8. TESTS FOR THE TONGUES MOVEMENT 89
  Harold Lindsell

9. A PROPOSAL FOR THE TONGUES
  CONTROVERSY 101
  Clark Pinnock and Grant R. Osborne

BIBLIOGRAPHY 111

CONTENTS

INTRODUCTION: WHAT IS DEAD MAY ...
1. SOME QUESTIONS ... ...
   Robert W. Jenson
2. THE NEW CONSENSUS ... ...
   James W. ...
3. IN SEARCH OF THE ... TO THE ... ...
   ... ...
4. THE USE AND ABUSE OF HUMAN ... ...
   Thomas F. Kaufman ... ...
5. CONSCIENCE AND THE ... CONSCIENCE ... ...
   ... ...
6. SPEAKING OF ... IN ... ...
   Robert W. ...
7. SPEAKING IN TONGUES ... ...
   Dennis ... ...
8. THE CHARISMATIC MOVEMENT IN THE ... ...
   ... ...
9. TESTS FOR THE KINGDOM COVENANT IN ... ...
   Harold Lindsell ... ...
10. MEDICAL FOR THE FUTURE ... ...
    CONTROVERSY
    ... ...
    BIBLIOGRAPHY

Introduction

TONGUES: UPDATING SOME OLD ISSUES

The new Pentecostalism, with its controversial tongues-speaking and healings, is more popular than ever. In the past decade there has been a further acceleration of the movement, spearheaded in part by the Jesus People and the Catholic Pentecostals, and in part by best sellers.

Religious bookstores which once looked askance at selling Pentecostal writings across their counters now acclaim them as their top merchandise. The writings of Pat Boone, David Wilkerson, Mel Tari, and Maria von Trapp have made the charismatic movement acceptable in places where it was once a forbidden topic.

Charismatic study groups thrive in many evangelical churches that would not have suffered them to exist ten years ago. And some evangelical churches that were thriving ten years ago have been rent in schism because of such groups.

As we look at the issues that separate charismatic from noncharismatic evangelicals, a few things have changed in the past decade, but there are also old issues that remain as sharp as ever.

Chief of these is the common, if not quite universal, claim by Pentecostal leaders, that speaking in tongues is the definite sign of the baptism of the Spirit. The implication, of course, is that if you have not received the "baptism" signified by tongues, you are a second-class Christian and missing out on God's best for your life.

This delegates a host of noncharismatics, including Billy Graham, to a less spiritual status in Christendom. It can also easily wreck a church, if the pastor has not experienced the "blessing" while other leading members have—or vice versa.

The problem is that the apostle Paul plainly states that every believer is baptized into the Spirit of God at the time of conversion: "If any man have not the spirit of God, he is none of his" (Rom. 8:9).

There may be subsequent fillings, as the disciples themselves experienced (Acts 4:31). But Paul never admonishes Christians to pray to receive the baptism of the Spirit.

In some groups, Christians are subjected to great psychological pressures regarding this subject. "You certainly wouldn't want to miss God's best for your life, would you?" they are counseled. "You aren't 100 percent satisfied with your Christian life, are you?" We insist that there is no Scriptural warrant for this kind of emotional and psychological manipulation.

We are also concerned about the widespread practice in neo-Pentecostal circles of tutoring "second-blessing" seekers in tongues-speaking. No one tutored the disciples on the day of Pentecost. No one tutored Cornelius and his friends (Acts 10). And no one tutored the Ephesian followers of John the Baptist (Acts 19). There is not even any reason to believe that they had any prior inkling that they were about to break out praising God in an unknown language. The spontaneousness of the phenomenon was one indication that it was a genuine, if unexpected, work of the Holy Spirit. Let not Bible-trained Christians today go around coaxing naive believers in how to let their tongue and vocal cords stumble into heavenly realms. The sovereign Holy Spirit needs no priming.

But there is one area where we have noticed a softening of the evangelical position toward Pentecostalism.

It is in the recognition that the gift of tongues may be a legitimate gift of the Holy Spirit, even as listed in I Corinthians 12. More and more evangelical scholars today feel that the traditional, supposedly Biblical arguments for the cessation of the gifts after completion of the New Testament cannot be sustained by the Holy Scriptures.

The new stress is on the church as the body of Christ with its various members endowed by the Spirit with differing gifts. The gifts are "apportioned to each of us just as the Spirit chooses"

(I Cor. 12:11, Goodspeed). And who would rule out tongues as one of these gifts? Certainly Paul didn't.

If such a gift is used in line with the strictures of I Corinthians 14 and for the upbuilding of the Body of Christ (I Cor. 12:7) (not its destruction), it should be recognized as legitimate. But beware of imitations.

All evangelicals need to admit in practice as well as in theory that God is sovereign. He can still show His power as and when He pleases among His people. If He chooses to do miracles of healings and endow some of His servants with the special gift of tongues, let us not circumscribe Him. All we ask is that His name be glorified and His body edified.

But Paul's most emphatic word to the Corinthians was to covet the gift of love. And He meant that we should love both the charismatics and the noncharismatics. In keeping with the earlier chapters of that Epistle, he meant that the gift of love would heal the party spirit that was dividing the church.

The church of Corinth was racked by many problems, not unlike the church today. Dividing the church were matters of sensuality, divorce, women's lib, denominationalism, and tongues-speaking. To such a church Paul wrote: "If I have not love, I am nothing."

1

THE
NEW
CHARISMATICS
by James W. L. Hills

In the last few years, American Pentecostalism has entered "phase three."

New and entirely unexpected groups have been touched by the Pentecostal tide. Labels and definitions are changing. Striking new emphases are developing.

Phase one can be traced to the turn of the century. What is now known as "classical Pentecostalism" had its popular beginning in 1906, in Los Angeles's Azusa Street Mission. There were antecedent Pentecostal experiences in different parts of the nation. One occurred at Charles F. Parham's Bethel Bible College, Topeka, Kansas, in 1901, and some historians cite outpourings of the Spirit a few years earlier. But Azusa Street marked the real beginning of the worldwide Pentecostal movement.

Phase two may be dated from 1960. That was the year the secular press discovered what some churchmen had known for several years: that the Pentecostal experience—"the baptism of the Holy Spirit, with the evidence of tongues"—was no longer the exclusive province of the socially and economically depressed. The dramatic public revelation of its extensive acceptance by members of a suburban Episcopal congregation in California was hot copy.

The new extension of Pentecostalism was dubbed "neo-Pentecostalism," and it spread rapidly. Soon the nation was dotted with charismatic prayer groups, comprised mostly of members of "main-line" Protestant churches. They claimed to have found a new dimension in their Christian lives through the Pentecostal baptism.

11

The year to keep in mind for phase three is 1967. In that year the movement took off in two new directions. A Roman Catholic Pentecostal movement got underway, and the Jesus People movement came into being, a movement which is predominantly, though not ostentatiously, charismatic.

What stimuli produced these new directions?

As far as the Catholic Pentecostal movement is concerned, some would point to the Second Vatican Council as an important factor, a Council which, in the view of Catholic theologian Hans Küng, came four hundred years too late. During Vatican II Pope John had prayed for a new Pentecost in Roman Catholicism. The open window and the fresh breeze were more than most had bargained for. Breeze became gale. One priest, presently active and joyfully caught up in the Pentecostal renewal, protests that he has found, not an "ism" or a "movement," but *a new life*. "It was an eighty-year-old Pope who revolutionized my thinking," he affirms, and he adds, "He upset the church, praise God!"

The Jesus People? Even the young had by the thousands come to realize by 1967 the bankruptcy of the directions many of them were taking. Enough of the rebels, revolutionaries, and runaways had had bad trips, whether on radical philosophy, eastern metaphysics, drugs, or sex, to know that their restless search had yielded no satisfaction. They were ready to hear and heed the word that God loved them. The field was ripe and ready for harvest.

The Catholic Charismatics

The spiritual hunger of two laymen on the faculty of Duquesne University, Pittsburgh, Pennsylvania, was stimulated in the spring of 1966 when they realized they lacked the power of the early Christians to proclaim the gospel. They shared their concern with others on the faculty. Then, in August 1966, two young men in attendance at the National Cursillo Convention (a Catholic renewal movement born in Europe in the late 1940s) introduced into this circle a book which had intrigued them: David Wilkerson's *The Cross and the Switchblade*. Early in January 1967, contacts were made with Protestant charismatics in the Pittsburgh area. By February several Duquesne faculty members had received the Pentecostal baptism. By the middle of the month, at what is now known as "the Duquesne weekend," the experience had come to a group of students and faculty on a wider scale. Wilkerson's book was a major factor.

In the meantime news of the first Pittsburgh area startings had reached the University of Notre Dame, Notre Dame, Indiana. Home prayer meetings, encouraged and assisted by members of the Full Gospel Business Men's Fellowship, saw a number of Catholics receive the baptism. Shortly after Easter, what has been called in retrospect the "First Annual National Catholic Pentecostal Conference" was held on the Notre Dame campus. About 100 students, priests, and faculty members, chiefly from Notre Dame and Michigan State, were in attendance. The gathering drew considerable publicity. Such a gathering, now organized in detail, has been held annually ever since. Growth has been phenomenal. The 100 of 1967 had become 11,500 (including seven bishops and four hundred priests) by the time of the Sixth Conference of June 1972. By now the gathering was international in scope. Catholic Pentecostalism was a vigorous, established fact.

The scope of the movement is such that it has been necessary to conduct special conferences for leaders in the movement. The first of these, held in January 1969, drew a modest fifty people. The second was attended by three hundred, the third by more than five hundred. Regional leaders' conferences were instituted. Steve Clark and Ralph Martin, two laymen active in the movement from its beginning, have been active teachers in these. Attendance built up. Over one thousand found their way to the Third Regional Conference, held in New Jersey. The concern of this conference was the danger of over-emphasizing spiritual experience at the expense of the fruits of the Spirit, especially love.

Yet the Catholic movement must not be seen as one which flits from conference to conference. Prayer groups had proliferated to such an extent around the country that it was found necessary to establish a "communication center" at Notre Dame, in 1969, specifically to serve the Catholic charismatic renewal. The center publishes a Directory of Catholic Charismatic Prayer Groups. The current issue (June 1972) lists nearly 550 groups in the United States, blanketing all the states—only Alaska is missing. Charismatic prayer groups are listed for twenty-seven other countries, suggesting again, the international nature of the movement.

The *Pastoral Newsletter,* a mimeographed sheet which in the early days reported developments in the movement, has since become *New Covenant,* an attractive thirty-six-page monthly magazine with a growing circulation. Ralph Martin serves as editor.

The spring of 1972 saw the establishment of the nation's first nonterritorial Catholic Pentecostal parish, the Community of the Holy Spirit, in St. Charles, Illinois. Bishop Arthur J. O'Neill of Rockford, Illinois, established the parish, with the Rev. William F. McMahon as pastor. Membership is open to Catholics outside the Rockford diocese and to non-Catholic Christians, though Father McMahon cannot act as their pastor. Bishop O'Neill sees the establishment of the parish as benefiting the whole church.

The American Catholic bishops decided in 1969 to allow the charismatic renewal within the Catholic Church to have free course. Bishop Joseph C. McKinney, Auxiliary Bishop of Grand Rapids, likes the movement's emphasis on the centrality of commitment to Christ. In his opinion, 90 percent of the bishops see the movement as a good thing.

Edward D. O'Connor, associate professor of theology at the University of Notre Dame, is the theologian of the movement. His is a strong Roman orientation, believing the Roman Church alone is fully authentic. Like the bishops generally, he has a strong concern for traditional patterns and a concern lest religious experience be substituted for religious doctrine.

This concern was evidenced at the Sixth International Conference in June 1972. Protestants in attendance ("separated brethren") were forbidden to receive Communion. One Irish priest felt outraged and fulminated: "Christians who came hundreds of miles, even thousands, to join in loving fellowship in the Spirit of Jesus were immediately divided at the altar. . . . The apostles were not 'roman catholics,' nor was the lady at the well. Was this granting maximum freedom to the Spirit of love? Belfast walls rose up at Notre Dame at that moment."

It is especially disturbing to Protestant evangelicals to find Mary honored at times as Mediatrix, and to hear of cases where tongues are interpreted as a "Hail Mary."

Within the Catholic Pentecostal movement there is a strong sense of community. Not surprisingly this has found expression in some well-organized communities. The Rev. John Randall has seen an inner-city parish, St. Patrick's of Providence, Rhode Island, come alive through the influence of the charismatic Word of God Community which was integrated into the life of the parish. The heart of the action is a weekly prayer meeting which draws six to seven hundred people. The charismatic community has stimulated the reopening of a parish school, fostered social action efforts, and revived what had become known as a dying parish.

Joy, praise, deepening of the prayer life, a love of the Scriptures—these are some of the positive fruits of the movement. They could eventually take care of un-Biblical excesses.

The Jesus People

According to Edward Plowman, "historian of the movement" (*Time*), the Jesus movement, like the Catholic Pentecostal movement, got its start in 1967. Some of the hippies of Haight-Ashbury, San Francisco, discovered Jesus Christ and the Bible that year. Today the Jesus People are a force to be reckoned with. Not always understood or appreciated by the "straights" within the established churches, they have made their presence keenly felt on the streets, at the radical political rallies, at the rock festivals, in the coffee houses, and through the underground press.

The milieu out of which they emerged as people transformed by the love of God was a society marked by widespread breakdown of home life, and conventional churches unwilling even to listen. They might be regarded as the products of moral relativism and a God-is-dead theology. They were the rejects of society, so they created their own society, and rotted there, pursuing their dead-end pursuits until, finally—some say it was a spontaneous work of God—Jesus found them. Duane Pederson, founder of the *Hollywood Free Paper,* takes credit for coining the name "Jesus People Movement."

Is the Jesus movement charismatic? If so, to what extent? This is a fair question to ask. Unlike many neo-Pentecostals, Protestant and Catholic, there is not a great deal of talk about speaking in tongues. For that matter, the Jesus People do not talk much about doctrine at all. The one consuming passion that drives them is Jesus Christ. They have popularized the "one way" symbol, the clenched fist with index finger extended heavenward: Jesus is the One Way. They have little time for other matters. Jesus Christ is all that matters. Hence it is not surprising if the tongues question is not even raised.

This is in marked contrast with the neo-Pentecostals of Protestant circles, where one is made much aware of the phenomenon of glossolalia. In much of the literature extensive articles deal with the subject Biblically, theologically, psychologically, linguistically. The articles not only defend the practice—they encourage it and often give recipelike instructions for coming into the experience. One can only conclude that, at least in many cases, the neo-Pentecostal is extremely self-conscious about his gift.

But the Jesus People are too busy with a multitude of ministries for this. They are engaged in outreach of all types. They are keen on balanced Bible study, often looking to a Christ-centered "straight" as teacher. Their communes are not usually a means of withdrawal but of outreach. Their coffee houses are centers of Jesus rap for their peers. They have learned from the radical underground movement the power of the press, and their publications are aggressively evangelistic. They have discovered the bookstore ministry. They have developed specialty ministries to young Jews, to the drug culture, to college students, and to the beach crowd.

Even a cursory survey of the literature of the movement confirms the overriding purpose: to get people to Jesus Christ rather than to an experience. Almost nothing is said on the subject of Spirit baptism. For that, one must turn to the literature of the classical Pentecostals, to the publications of such firms as Logos (Plainfield, New Jersey), which serves especially the main-line Protestant Pentecostals, to the Full Gospel Business Men's Fellowship, or to the publications of the Catholic Pentecostals. Holy Spirit baptism is mentioned at times in the testimonies of the Jesus People in their newspapers. But one does not get the impression at all that the experience as such is being promoted.

Instead, you hear, for example, that *The Jesus Paper,* published by Bruce P. Jackson, of Washington, D.C., distributed more than fifteen thousand New Testaments in 1972, mostly to new Christians. Or that nine thousand letters of testimony were received from readers in the same period, many naming the publication as the means of their conversion.

Nor are the papers bashful or subtle in their approach. They avidly challenge the philosophies and presuppositions of the radical left, take up the cause of women's lib where they feel the dignity and rights of women are being violated, peddle their literature on the streets—and all to the end of proclaiming the power of the love of God to set people free.

Quietly Charismatic

Is the Jesus People movement charismatic? William F. Willoughby, religious news editor of the *Washington Star,* has done as much reporting on the Jesus People as any secular newsman. In his considered opinion a minimum of 70 percent and as high as 85 percent of the Jesus People movement is charismatic, with most of these having the experience of glossolalia and, in many cases, other gifts of the Spirit. Yet Willoughby says he has yet to run across a group of the Jesus People who insist upon an individual speaking in tongues.

Another source, a former missionary who maintains contact with one hundred Jesus People ministries in forty-eight states, unequivocally states that most of the centers are charismatic, though they do not stress it.

My own studies seem to confirm these opinions.

Is there any relationship between the Catholic Pentecostal and the Jesus People movements? Any relationship is only incidental. Though both movements originated about the same time, each was born out of a distinct cultural setting and has developed within that setting. The leaders in the Catholic movement tell me that they have had either no contact with the Jesus People movement, or at best limited contact.

Protestant Neo-Pentecostalism

How is the neo-Pentecostal movement doing among main-line Protestants? Very well, thank you!

Among the Lutherans, the American Lutheran Church saw

most of the action in the early 1960s. Controversy which erupted in 1963 was quieted down by the issuance of guidelines. Then the experience touched Missouri Synod circles in 1967. Several of its ministers were defrocked because of public statements on the issue. Within the Lutheran Church of America the issue has proved to be divisive and a special commission was appointed in 1972 to study the matter. The penetration into Lutheran circles is suggested by the fact that more than ten thousand attended the First International Lutheran Conference on the Holy Spirit held in Minneapolis, Minnesota, in August 1972.

In 1970 the General Assembly of the United Presbyterian Church in the U.S.A. issued its report on "The Work of the Holy Spirit." Reflecting two years of careful study, it has been hailed as one of the best official statements on the charismatic renewal and has brought about considerable growth in the movement. A National Presbyterian Conference on the Holy Spirit held in January 1972, in Saint Louis, drew 150 ministers. A "Charismatic Communion of Presbyterian Ministers" has attracted 350 members and is growing. It is estimated that between 10,000 and 15,000 members of the United Presbyterian Church and the Presbyterian Church in the U.S. have received the Pentecostal baptism.

These two denominations are only representative of the growth noted in other main-line denominations.

The most significant development for Pentecostalism on the international scene is the establishment by the Vatican (Secretariat for Promoting Christian Unity) of a five-year dialogue on the theology and experiential elements of Pentecostalism with representatives of classical and neo-Pentecostalism. Cochairmen of the first session, held in Zurich, Switzerland, in June 1972, were David Du Plessis, the "Mr. Pentecost" who has been instrumental in opening doors for the experience in ecumenical circles, and Father Kilian McConnell, executive director of the Institute for Ecumenical and Cultural Research, Collegeville, Minnesota.

Some Final Observations

1. At the present time a refreshing wave of evangelicalism is sweeping the churches. Often the stimulus is from the outside. Evangelicals are finding anew the love of God, the deepening of

their lives through the Word of God, new energy for evangelism, and an awareness of the power of the Spirit. Much of this is noncharismatic in character. Yet the stimulus in some measure is coming from Pentecostal sources, especially with respect to the spiritual hunger that is being created and the joy and spirit of worship that is being released.

2. Pentecostalism is chiefly experience-centered. Some evangelicals, particularly those of Reformed background, are uneasy about this. A new journal, *Present Truth,* published in California, takes a stand against Pentecostalism in all its forms, but especially as it has appeared in the Jesus People movement and in the Catholic Church. But *experience* of the gospel is an essential additive to the doctrine of the gospel, providing that the experience is formed by and subject to the correction of the Scriptures.

3. Most evangelicals continue to have problems with the Biblical exegesis and theological assumptions of Pentecostalism, especially on the matter of Holy Spirit baptism. John R. W. Stott's small book *The Baptism and Fullness of the Holy Spirit* would probably speak for most evangelicals. Stott does not close the door on the possibility or authenticity of "special experiences" today, as dispensationalists sometimes do. But he points out the responsibility of all believers, whether or not they have had unusual experiences of the Holy Spirit, to be filled with, to be led by, and to walk in the Spirit.

4. I can most certainly afford a generous, open attitude toward the movement insofar as the fruits of the Spirit are manifest. Beyond that, I have the responsibility to exercise discernment. God has, more than once, used surprising instruments to bring renewal to His people.

2

FACING
THE ISSUES
OF TONGUES
by Stanley Gundry

Susan Meissner, Seattle leader of the Jesus People Army: *I speak in tongues. It changed my life from a bashful farm girl to a powerful revolutionary.*

Singer Pat Boone: *When I run out of English and find myself groping self-consciously for the way to express myself, now I find complete freedom as the Holy Spirit, in this unfettered, infinitely expressive prayer language helps me to communicate directly with my Heavenly Father through Jesus Christ my Lord.*

News Report: *Notre Dame University–11,000 Catholic Pentecostals meet in annual conference. Minneapolis– 8,000 Lutheran Pentecostals gather in meeting.*

No alert Christian can afford to ignore the many questions raised by the current interest in glossolalia or speaking in tongues. The growth of the classic Pentecostal denominations in the twentieth century has been phenomenal in itself, but in the last ten or fifteen years the neo-Pentecostal or charismatic movement has penetrated widely. Today it is found in main-line Protestant churches, Roman Catholic circles, among the so-called Jesus People and on the campuses of Christian colleges and seminaries. In fact, rare is the evangelical church or organization that has not faced or is not now confronting the issue of tongues-speaking. Individual Christians who have not had the tongues experience are wondering if they are missing out on the secret of spiritual power.

What is the teaching of Pentecostalism, both old and new, that has set Christendom abuzz with more than glossolalia? Actually, the question is not an easy one, for there seem to be several streams of thought in the movement as a whole which might inclusively be called "Pentecostalism."

Generally the earlier Pentecostalism taught that a second experience called "baptism in the Holy Spirit" should follow one's conversion, with speaking in tongues as the necessary and inevitable evidence that it has taken place. While not necessary to salvation, this baptism is thought to be something every believer should experience in order to realize fully the potential of the Holy Spirit's ministry in his life.

The more recent charismatics, however, do not necessarily accept this view. Some seem to speak of Spirit baptism as though it were simply a decisive moment of dedication to God which might be accompanied by tongues. A Catholic Pentecostal writes, "The common denominator of the pentecostal experience seems to be inspired praise of the Lord, *either* in one's own language *or* in tongues" (italics added).

Others appear to be saying that though one speaks in tongues when he receives the baptism, the permanent gift of speaking in tongues is something God may or may not give to a believer who has received the baptism.

In other words there is no universally held view among Pentecostals or charismatics on glossolalia. Even so, all such groups accept tongues-speaking as a valid gift of God. Most give it high priority as a quickening experience, which they regard as "the normal Christian life in the New Testament assemblies" and "normal in the 1970s."

This lack of agreement among tongues-speakers themselves makes it difficult to discuss the subject in a manner fair to all and in a way which avoids stereotypes or caricatures. The difficulty is compounded by the fact that those at the opposite poles of the discussion tend to become emotionally involved. Understandably they feel that the validity of their walk with God is being challenged. They also are excited about what they regard as climactic experience in their Christian lives.

Although it is good that recent attitudes and discussions have tended to be more moderate and conciliatory, much of the discussion has tended to ignore some very basic questions. As a non-tongues-speaker, I would like to raise some of these questions in a very candid way, but hopefully without contention with brothers and sisters in Christ who may hold other viewpoints. The goal will be to clarify issues, promote mutual understanding and a fuller appreciation of God's will in this important matter.

Let us focus on six crucial questions:

1. *What or who should serve as the final authority in the judgment of this issue?*

The obvious answer would seem to be that it should be God speaking in His Word, the Scriptures. This ideal is all too easily short-circuited, for the temptation is ever present to use the Bible to support one's preconceptions. Even more subtle is the tendency to interpret the Bible in the light of one's experience rather than to interpret experience in the light of the Bible. Since both the older and newer Pentecostalism tend to be experience-oriented, this becomes especially crucial on the question of tongues.

A tongues-speaker recently wrote the editor of *Christianity Today,* "You cannot give fair treatment to a gift from God which you neither believe in or have experienced." This person has really said that tongues-speaking is not subject to critical examination in the light of Scripture. Yet to say that the one who has spoken in tongues is the only one qualified to comment on the subject is to assume the experience is a gift of God and to put the subjective above the Scripture.

Since what has happened to the glossolalist is no more exempt from the judgment of the Word of God than any other aspect of the Christian life, the tongues-speaker should be willing to examine his experience in the light of Scripture. Only in this way can he determine whether or not his experience is the same as that spoken of as tongues in the New Testament.

The tongues encounter is apparently very real to those who have had it. But that is not the question. Rather, what kind of an experience was it; what is Spirit baptism and how does an emphasis on glossolalia square with the priorities of Christian living as carefully spelled out in the New Testament? Is it the same as the phenomenon experienced in the first-century church? These are the real questions and only the New Testament can answer them.

2. *Is speaking in tongues alone sufficient to validate a person's Christian experience and theological beliefs?*

The question is raised because there is a tendency to assume that a person who has spoken in tongues must be a Christian and that his basic theology and practice must therefore be regarded as beyond criticism. Some readily accessible facts and sober considerations should bring matters into proper perspective. Common sense recognizes that a tongues experience can be counterfeited; indeed many Pentecostalists are among the first to recognize this. Furthermore, instances of ecstatic utterance are not uncommon in non-Christian religions.

In other words, tongues are not a uniquely Christian occurrence. Then what about liberal Protestants and Roman Catholics who have spoken in tongues? Is the fact that a person from a liberal Protestant theological tradition has spoken in tongues reason to ignore the unbelief inherent in that liberal theology?

The same can be asked of Roman Catholic charismatics. In the words of a Catholic parish newspaper, Roman Catholics in the Pentecostal movement are "learning from their experience about effective use of the sacraments" (understood in the Roman Catholic sense). Other Catholic Pentecostals testify that the charismatic experience has deepened their devotion to Mary. Catholic charismatic leaders and members of the hierarchy are appealing to the movement to remain in the Roman Church and "to remain faithful to the leadership of the papacy."

Just as charismatics from liberal Protestantism must face up to the theological aberrations of liberalism, so Catholic charismatics who hope to remain in good standing in their church must be willing to face up to the issues raised by the church's theological deviations in the areas of justification, the sacrifice of the Mass, penance, papal infallibility, the doctrines of Mary and the authority of church and tradition alongside Scripture.

This is not to say that many of these charismatics in both Romanism and liberal Protestantism may not be saved. But the mere fact of their having spoken in tongues is not proof of their salvation; and those who are genuinely saved must be willing to go on and face the serious theological errors of their churches.

3. *Was speaking in tongues intended to be an experience that*

every believer should have, an experience to be sought after as the ideal of Christian living?

Though some in the movement would agree with the charismatic who recently said, "I . . . was baptized with the Holy Spirit long before I even heard of tongues," many if not most Pentecostals place a high priority on tongues-speaking as the desired Christian norm. Specifically this third question seeks to examine the frequent Pentecostal insistence that Spirit baptism is a second experience to be sought after conversion with tongues-speaking as the necessary and inevitable evidence of the baptism.

That speaking in tongues is the evidence of Spirit baptism seems unlikely from a comparison of I Corinthians 12:13 and 12:30. Paul and *all* the Corinthian believers had been baptized by one Spirit into the Body of Christ (12:13), but all had *not* spoken in tongues (12:30)!

This also suggests, contrary to Pentecostal theory, that baptism by the Spirit takes place *once at conversion* when the believer is incorporated into the Body of Christ, not as an experience to be desired later (cf. also Gal. 3:26-28). This is to be distinguished from being filled with the Spirit which may recur on numerous occasions.

Filling is not necessarily associated with tongues-speaking, but more with the Holy Spirit's empowering control. Nowhere in the New Testament do we find a priority put on speaking in tongues as an important element of one's Christian walk.

It is incredible that Paul should ignore it in his discussions of Christian life and character in Romans, Galatians, Ephesians, Philippians, and Colossians if speaking in tongues really has the importance which charismatics attach to it. Paul's only discussion of tongues is in the context of the problems the practice had created and in which he suggests that tongues do not have the highest priority (12:31—13:1).

Tongues-seekers and -speakers should candidly face these questions: "Does the New Testament attach the same priority and significance to speaking in tongues that I do? Or are the priorities for Christian character to be found elsewhere?"

4. *Was speaking in tongues a gift intended only for the early church, or are later manifestations of the phenomenon possible?*

Some opponents of glossolalia argue very dogmatically that I Corinthians 13:8-10 proves that a valid exercise of tongues is impossible today. The usual argument is that tongues were to cease (13:8) when the New Testament was complete ("when the perfect comes," 13:10).

Such dogmatism rests on a shaky foundation. The interpretation is highly disputable since "the perfect" is not defined and the time of cessation is otherwise unspecified. Theological dogmatism should be reserved for less debatable points.

However, having said that, perhaps it is significant that even in the first-century church, speaking in tongues seems to occupy a less and less significant place the further from Pentecost one moves. This is probably tied to the nature of tongues as a confirmatory sign for the young church.

While unwarranted dogmatism should be avoided, it does seem appropriate to question the assertion that speaking in tongues is to be expected as a permanent and normal feature of the life of the church, either corporately or individually.

5. *Was speaking in tongues in the experiences of the first-century church a speaking in unlearned foreign languages or an ecstatic utterance lacking those characteristics common to intelligible spoken languages, or both?*

Pentecostalists argue, and many non-Pentecostalists agree, that at least in I Corinthians 12—14 the tongues spoken of are ecstatic utterances. In fact, most recent discussions of tongues have assumed that tongues include ecstatic utterance with the result that the very strong evidence for understanding *tongues* in the New Testament to refer exclusively to intelligible foreign languages has been by-passed. Though discussion of the evidence and opposing arguments could become quite technical the following considerations seem inescapable.

a. Usually in Greek literature and in the New Testament, *tongue* refers to meaningful human speech.

b. The Word *interpretation* (used seven times in I Corinthians 12—14) in such a context normally refers to translation of intelligible human languages.

c. In Acts 2:6-11 Luke clearly intends speaking in tongues to refer to speaking in foreign languages. Since Luke and Paul were co-workers, it is likely that Luke is reflecting Paul's understanding of tongues, an understanding which would be expressed in I Corinthians 12—14.

d. But what about I Corinthians 12—14? Many interpreters feel that ecstatic utterance is clearly implied here. But look again. In 13:1 Paul writes of the "tongues of men and angels." It is claimed this suggests that tongues are a heavenly or angelic language which Paul spoke. But Paul does not claim to have spoken an angelic language. He says "if " and the usage of *tongues* in this verse actually presumes their intelligibility and viability as languages.

As for 14:2 which is supposed to point toward ecstatic utterance, it need not mean any more than that without translation the value of speaking in tongues is limited to the speaker's emotions since no one, including the speaker, understands (cf. 14:9). For this reason Paul advises the tongues-speaker to pray for the gift of interpretation (14:13) and commands him to be silent in the assembly when no one is present who can interpret the tongue (14:28).

It is the absence of an interpreter, not the ecstatic nature of the tongue, which makes the tongue unintelligible. On the Day of Pentecost interpreters were not needed because the audience was cosmopolitan, speaking many different languages. At Corinth, though, the audience was local and without translation a tongue might appear as gibberish (cf. 14:6-12, 16-18, 23).

Certainly 14:10-11 should make it perfectly clear than when Paul speaks of the gift of tongues, he refers to miraculous speaking in unlearned human languages. "There are, perhaps, a great many kinds of languages in the world, and no kind is without meaning. If then I do not know the meaning of the language, I shall be to the one who speaks a barbarian, and the one who speaks will be a barbarian to me" (NASB). Therefore the one who speaks in a tongue should pray that he may interpret (14:13).

If the New Testament gift of tongues was the gift of speaking in unlearned foreign languages, the implications for today are clear. Since very few tongues-speakers claim to be speaking foreign languages, and since there are even fewer instances of speaking in unlearned languages, nearly all contemporary "tongues-speaking" fails to qualify as tongues-speaking (unlearned, intelligible foreign languages) in the New Testament sense. Most claims to glossolalia could be rejected on this basis alone.

6. *If the contemporary tongues-speaking experience is not the New Testament gift of speaking unlearned foreign languages, what is it?*

Here one must exercise extreme care, for once it has been determined that at least most present-day glossolalia are not the same as that exercised in the early church, Scripture has no more to say. If not the New Testament gift, the nature of the present phenomena must be determined on other grounds. Different studies have been made and all the evidence is not yet in. However, at least five possibilities exist to explain different situations.

In some cases the tongues-speaker may be putting on an act —faking. In others, a demonic influence may be operative. While we would prefer to think that such cases are rare and should leave the judgment to God unless the indications are perfectly clear, it would be naive to refuse to allow these two as possibilities.

In some instances there is reason to think that the tongues-speaker's experience is self-induced, produced by the verbal repetition of certain formula words or by turning the voice loose until self-restraint is broken and the sought-for speech occurs. Closely related are the expressions of those who may have this verbal response to a spiritual crisis because previous teaching or example has taught them to expect to have this response; in other words, their experience fulfills their expectations.

Perhaps many who have spoken unintelligible utterances in moments of spiritual ecstasy in this manner have attempted to give voice to emotions that seemed incapable of normal rational expression. In such instances the individual should recognize that the occurence is not the gift of tongues and examine his priorities, not allowing the experience to become an end in itself.

In any case those involved in the tongues phenomena must critically examine their experience and ask themselves the question, "Has an emotional experience that produces a temporary euphoria been allowed to supersede the real work the Spirit desires to do in my life?"

Believers are admonished to "be filled with the Spirit," to

"walk by the Spirit," and to "be led by the Spirit" (Eph. 5:18; Gal. 5:16-25). These phrases speak of His empowering, control, and direction. To the extent that the Spirit is given this place in a Christian's life the fruit of the Spirit will be produced (Gal. 5:22-23).

The Spirit's work does not necessarily come with sensational or highly emotional manifestations. In fact, the expectation of tangible, sensational manifestations of the Spirit's work (such as tongues) may be an indication of spiritual immaturity and a substitute for the real work He wants to do in us (I Cor. 6:19-20)!

The call that comes to us all, Pentecostalist and non-Pentecostalist, is to present ourselves to God (Rom. 6 and 12), to be filled and led by His Spirit, not to seek or expect to speak in tongues.

3

THE USE
AND ABUSE
OF TONGUES
(Part 1)
by Theodore H. Epp and John I. Paton

The Corinthian church was a church with severe internal problems. It was undoubtedly the most carnal church to which Paul wrote (I Cor. 3:1). And yet, they were enriched by Christ "in all utterance and in all knowledge." Paul covers the subject of knowledge in the early chapters, and the subject of speech or utterance in chapters 12, 13, and 14. These Corinthian believers were in no way inferior to other local church groups with regard to the special gifts of the Spirit (I Cor. 1:7). Nevertheless, with all these advantages there were enough individuals in that church misusing their privileges to characterize the whole group as "babes in Christ" (I Cor. 3:1).

It is very evident from reading chapters 12, 13, and 14 of I Corinthians (sometimes known as "The Spirituals"), that the tongues-gift was given a very high place in the thinking of many of the Corinthian believers. That the inspired apostle did not share this view with them is also clear from this same section.

Apparently the Corinthian believers regarded the gift of tongues as the best of the miracle gifts, and counted those exercising it as a sort of spiritual aristocracy. This gift was so abused among them that they were in danger of repelling other believers as well as unbelievers who came into the church services (I Cor. 14:23).

The Nature of the Tongues-Gift at Corinth

Some Bible expositors think that there is a marked difference between the gift of tongues in Acts and the gift of tongues in I Corinthians. The position held by many is that in the Book of Acts the gift of tongues was the ability given a person to speak

31

foreign languages without his having learned them, while the gift in I Corinthians was that of ecstatic utterances. Some translators have even used that expression in I Corinthians wherever the gift of tongues is mentioned. Others believe that ecstatic utterances characterize the gift from the beginning, even in the Book of Acts. This, of course, will not stand up under examination as we have seen.

Others, and we are among them, believe that the gift of tongues is the same in Acts and in I Corinthians.

It should be said here that the word "unknown," which is used as an adjective qualifying the word "tongue" or "tongues" in I Corinthians 14, is not in the original. This is clear in the King James Version where the word "unknown" is in italics. Furthermore, there is no good reason for the word "unknown" to have been added.

The same words are used in I Corinthians to describe the gift as are used in the Book of Acts. Compare such passages as Acts 10:46; 19:6; and I Corinthians 14:5. The terminology is identical in the two books. And there is nothing in the context of I Corinthians that would suggest anything other than languages. Verse 1 of chapter 13 is sometimes pointed to as a proof of ecstatic utterances, but as one of the great Greek expositors of a past generation stated: "The 'tongues of men' must mean the tongues spoken by men in general if language is to have its natural sense." The same would hold true for the tongues or languages of angels.

The word "tongue" appears eight times in the fourteenth chapter of I Corinthians. With one exception (v. 9), this singular form of the word refers to the gift of tongues. In verse 9 the physical organ itself is meant. Paul said, "So likewise ye, except ye utter by the tongue words easy to be understood, how shall it be known what is spoken? for ye shall speak into the air." The plural form appears eight times also. Seven of the occurrences have to do with the gift of tongues. In verse 21 where the word "tongues" does not have reference to the gift of tongues, it, nevertheless, has to do with foreign languages. Now, how will we explain this changing from the singular to the plural with reference to this gift of the Holy Spirit if the gift of tongues is the gift of ecstatic utterances? There is no problem if we recognize that the gift of tongues is the gift to speak in a foreign language not previously known to the one speaking in tongues. Furthermore, the result of this gift is "words." These are not jumbled words or gibberish, but words "easy to be understood" (v. 9).

Consider the word "barbarian" in verse 11. This has no reference to a person's theology or religion. It is simply a reference to his language. The ancient Egyptians considered anyone who could not speak Egyptian to be a foreigner. The Greeks picked up this same bit of racial snobbery and called anyone who could not speak Greek a "barbarian," or in our language, a foreigner. So Paul says in verse 11 that if someone were to speak to him in a language which he, Paul, could not understand, each would be a barbarian or foreigner to the other. On the basis of this fact, Dr. Robert L. Thomas of Talbot Theological Seminary says in the May 1963, issue of the *King's Business*: "If this verse referred to a man's incoherent, inarticulate sounds which no living person could understand, it would not make him a foreigner, but a babbler. The contrary would be true, however, if he spoke a foreign language."

In the light of these facts, it seems more reasonable to understand the gift of tongues in Corinth to be the same as that at Pentecost, namely the ability to speak in a foreign language not previously learned by the tongues-speaker.

Limitations of the Gift

The gift of tongues is definitely limited as to its ministry. This is clear from the contrast which Paul draws between the gift of prophecy and the gift of tongues. He encourages believers to seek spiritual gifts but to prefer the gift of prophecy over that of tongues (I Cor. 14:1). We have already indicated that prophecy has various elements, one being that of telling forth the Word of God (I Cor. 14:3). In this it was closely related to what we call Bible teaching. Another element was the power to predict events and conditions (Acts 11:27-28). A third element, essential at that time when all the New Testament was not yet given, was the power to receive new truth from God (I Cor. 14:30).

A gift of this nature was necessary to help God's people grow in grace and in the knowledge of our Lord Jesus Christ. In contrast to this, the tongues-gift limited a man to some special experience with

God but with no service to the church, unless he could interpret or an interpreter were present.

This is the reason why the Holy Spirit, through Paul, said that the man who had the prophetic gift was greater than the one who spoke in a foreign tongue. The source of each gift was the same —the Holy Spirit. The service rendered, however, was not the same. The gift of prophecy far outstripped the gift of tongues in this regard.

Moreover, lest anyone should set a higher value on the personal benefits that might come through speaking in a foreign tongue, the apostle goes on to declare that even in the realm of communion and prayer the gift is limited. The man who prayed in a foreign tongue prayed in the Spirit, but his mind—his understanding—was not helped. He could not express to himself what he had felt in the experience of prayer, much less pass it on to others. Paul did not think such an experience was worth repeating, for he says, "I will pray with the spirit, and I will pray with the understanding also" (I Cor. 14:15).

The gift of tongues was limited in its distribution. It was not available to all believers. "Do all speak with tongues?" the apostle asks (I Cor. 12:30). The answer is obvious. They do not! The gifts were distributed to the believers according to the will of the Spirit of God. None of the miracle gifts was common to all believers. Most certainly the gift of tongues was not given to each believer in the Corinthian church or any other New Testament church. So far as importance goes, if the list in I Corinthians 12 is a standard in this respect, the gift of tongues was not first but last (v. 28).

This does not support the teaching that the initial sign or evidence of the presence of the Holy Spirit in a life is the gift of tongues. Furthermore, regardless of whether one believes the gift of tongues to be foreign languages or ecstatic utterances in I Corinthians, the limitation of its distribution still holds. Not all received it. The baptism of the Holy Spirit was for all believers, and according to I Corinthians 12:13 this was realized; but not every believer spoke in tongues. These two things should not be made identical, for they are not the same. The baptism of the Spirit inducts believers into the Body of Christ, and every believer is a member of that Body. Few of them, however, have ever spoken in tongues.

The distribution of these miracle gifts was under the direction of the Holy Spirit (I Cor. 12:7-11). To teach that all believers will speak in tongues, or should speak in tongues, contradicts this very plain passage. Nowhere in the Scriptures are believers told specifically to seek the gift of tongues. They are admonished to seek spiritual gifts, but rather that they might prophesy. Thus the gift of tongues is played down in this inspired admonition (I Cor. 14:1).

Rules Governing the Gift of Tongues

In I Corinthians we have these three chapters devoted to the subject of spiritual gifts. The fourteenth, which is the longest of the three, deals with the limitations of a gift, rules covering its use, and severe warnings concerning its abuse. Surely any earnest believer who wants to please the Lord would not treat this matter lightly. Nether would he draw from this chapter conclusions contrary to its whole tone.

General Rules

There are two general rules. The first we have already touched on. It has to do with the fact that the apostle Paul encouraged the Corinthians to seek spiritual gifts, but stated a preference for prophecy rather than for tongues. It should be sufficient to say that anyone who claims to be directed by the Spirit of God, yet changes the divine order and emphasis in relation to these two gifts, is going contrary to the revealed will of God. No matter how much the Person and work of the Holy Spirit may be emphasized by such a person, if the Holy Spirit's instructions are brushed aside, He is dishonored and grieved.

The second general rule has to do with order in the meetings of God's people. Confusion and disorderliness are alien to the Spirit of God (I Cor. 14:26, 33). A good deal of confusion and disharmony marked the meetings in Corinth as a result of speaking in tongues.

Specific Rules

1. There are a number of these, one of which is found in

I Corinthians 14:6. Paul said, "Now, brethren, if I come unto you speaking with tongues, what shall I profit you, except I shall speak to you either by revelation, or by knowledge, or by prophesying, or by doctrine?" This is saying in just so many words that Bible truth must be given if the tongues-gift is employed in the way God intends it to be employed. It is the Word of God which benefits the hearers. It is through the Word that the Spirit of God works in the hearts of His people.

A good question to ask ourselves with regard to any claim of speaking in tongues is this: "Is the Word of God expounded as a result of this gift? Are people being built up in the faith once for all delivered to the saints? Is Christ being exalted?" If the answer to these questions is No, then it is a real question if the Spirit of God is in the tongues-speaking.

2. The tongues-gift should be used for the edification of the whole church and not limited to the personal benefit of the man with the gift (I Cor. 14:2, 12). Spirit-given gifts are not the play-things of men. They are not for selfish ends, but for the upbuilding of the Body of Christ. The believer is not his own; he has been bought with a price. Any spiritual gift he receives is not for his private entertainment or benefit, but for the good of all believers with whom he has contact.

3. A third rule is that in a group where all, including the tongues-speaker, spoke the same mother tongue, the one speaking in tongues must either be his own interpreter or someone else must interpret for him. Otherwise, the tongues-speaker was to remain silent (I Cor. 14:28).

What a boon this gift would be to foreign missionaries who must spend months and even years in learning a new language. Some of them, in fact, have to learn several new languages in the course of their missionary work.

At the turn of this century some enthusiastic and earnest Christians went out to the mission fields with the firm conviction that they had the gift of tongues. They believed it would not be necessary for them to learn the mother tongue of the people to whom they would minister. These would-be missionaries were sadly disillusioned. Many of them became spiritual wrecks as a result of their disappointment. The fault did not lie with God, but with them, and those teachers who had misinterpreted the Scriptures with regard to the gift of tongues.

4. Another specific rule was that private praying in a tongue was not to be encouraged unless the one who prayed understood what he was praying about. The standard Paul laid down was that one should pray not only with the human spirit, but with the understanding also (I Cor. 14:14-15).

5. A definite order was to be maintained when tongues-speaking was used in a public meeting. No more than three tongues-speakers were to take part in any one service, and then only one at a time with someone to interpret (I Cor. 14:27). Since there was to be only one interpreter, this in itself would tend to keep several tongues-speakers from trying to speak at the same time. By this means confusion would be eliminated and one of the disorders accompanying the zeal of those employing the gift would be corrected.

6. We have already considered the fact that if a believer employed the gift of tongues he was to give Bible truth. A fresh look at this will help us to see that in Corinth, in the day this admonition was given, more than one miraculous gift would be needed in order to protect believers from false prophets. Paul said, "If I come unto you speaking with tongues, what shall I profit you, except I shall speak to you either by revelation, or by knowledge, or by prophesying, or by doctrine?" (I Cor. 13:6).

Bible truth, or new truth from God, was to be given if the hearers were to be edified. In this way the gift of prophecy would be joined with the gift of tongues. This meant that not only would the rules governing tongues be employed, but also an additional rule governing prophecy would have to be followed.

This particular rule is given in verse 29: "Let the prophets speak two or three, and let the other judge." The function of a judge in this case would be the discerning of spirits, for in the days when the New Testament had not all been given, additional truth would be revealed from time to time. But with this went the danger of false doctrine being introduced. There needed to be a check on the teaching of the prophets lest evil spirits interject false teaching.

This judge, then, would be one who would try the spirits, and he would need for this the gift of the discerning of spirits.

In a situation of this nature three miracle gifts are needed—the gift of tongues, prophecy, and the discerning of spirits. Does not this indicate that if one miracle gift is to be used, several or even all of them are needed to keep the rest in balance? We hear much of the gift of tongues, but what of the other gifts? Very often in such circles Mark 16:17 is referred to as proof that the gift of tongues is a sign that shall follow believers. But why pick out that one gift and leave out the casting out of demons, the taking up of serpents, the drinking of deadly poison, or the healing of the sick? And, let us not overlook another gift spoken of in Matthew 10:8, that of raising the dead!

7. A seventh rule is found in verse 32. Here we are told that in the case of the prophets the spirits of the prophets are subject to the prophets. This principle applied to the tongues-speakers also. The expression of their gift was not beyond their control. It was their responsibility to see that they used it wisely and in an orderly way. Too often God is blamed for what is in reality the believer's own lack of restraint.

8. A very serious consequence to the use of tongues without an interpreter is dealt with in verses 21-23. This is a portion that has not always been clearly understood.

The apostle emphasizes in this chapter that spiritual gifts are to be used for the edification of the believers. Obviously there could be no edification if they could not understand the language being used. But what will the effect be upon unbelievers who attend the church services? This is the subject Paul deals with in these verses.

He says, "In the law it is written, With men of other tongues and other lips will I speak unto this people; and yet for all that will they not hear me, saith the Lord. Wherefore tongues are for a sign, not to them that believe, but to them that believe not: but prophesying serveth not for them that believe not, but for them which believe. If therefore the whole church be come together into one place, and all speak with tongues, and there come in those that are unlearned, or unbelievers, will they not say that ye are mad? But if all prophesy, and there come in one that believeth not, or one unlearned, he is convinced of all, he is judged of all: And thus are the secrets of his heart made manifest; and so falling down on his face he will worship God, and report that God is in you of a truth."

The first question we want to answer is this; "In what sense are tongues a sign to unbelievers?"

The answer lies in this portion. The "law" here is the Old Testament, and the part quoted is Isaiah 28:11-12. When the messages of the prophets were resisted by hard-hearted unbelievers among the Israelites, God warned them that He would judge them by sending foreign invaders into their land. These men would speak languages unknown to the Israelites, and the presence of these conquerors would be proof of God's retributive judgment upon His people who would not believe in spite of this sign. They would "not hear" the Lord. Consequently, the uninterpreted tongue was a judicial sign to unbelievers. The uninterpreted tongue would indicate judgment upon the unbelieving and would not be a means of leading them to a faith in Christ.

Now this was the very opposite of what God intended at Corinth. It stands to reason that the unbelievers who visited the meetings of the Christians in Corinth were not hardened against truth but were seeking spiritual help.

So far as the original Greek is concerned, the word for unbelievers in verse 22 is the same as the word for unbelievers in verse 23. But the context indicates that the unbeliever in verse 22 is of a different kind than that of verse 23. Tongues were a judicial sign against hardened unbelievers. But since the Corinthians in their meetings would not be dealing with hardened unbelievers, but with unbelievers who were apparently seeking spiritual help, by using the gifts of tongues without an interpreter present the Corinthians were misrepresenting God's attitude toward these lost persons. A further evil result of the uninterpreted tongue would be that the unbelievers attending the services would think God's people were mentally unbalanced.

Still others were adversely affected by the uninterpreted tongue. They are spoken of as the "unlearned" (v. 23). The word in the original had as its primary meaning a private person as contrasted to a public official. In this context it denotes a person or persons who, though saved, were "untaught" or "unlearned" so far as tongues were concerned. So, like the unbelievers of verse 23, these "unlearned" persons would consider the foreign language used by the tongues-speakers as mere gibberish and think the speakers were not emotionally stable.

God's purpose in the giving out of the gospel is to reach the unsaved and bring them to a saving knowledge of Christ, as well as to help the believers grow in grace and in the knowledge of their Lord. He does this by reaching the understanding through intelligible words and appealing to the conscience at the same time. God's Word is heard through the speaker, but if the speaker uses language that is not understood by his hearers, then God's purpose cannot be carried through. To declare that a person is judged (v. 24) means that his heart is searched by the Word and he is inwardly sifted. Each successive speaker in the assembly who speaks in the power of the Holy Spirit deepens the work of the Spirit in these individual hearts.

Verse 25 shows the third stage in this person's conversion if he is an unbeliever. The secrets of his heart are made manifest. In the first place there is revealed to him his true condition. According to verse 24 he stands self-condemned and sees his own thoughts, motives, and desires in their true light. He is awakened to his need and falls down before God.

9. Finally, women are forbidden to speak in the public assemblies. Connected as this thought is with the subject of tongues, it is very apparent that the women were not allowed to speak in tongues in the early church (I Cor. 14:34).

One is forced to admit in the light of these rules that although Paul says, "Forbid not to speak with tongues" (I Cor. 14:39), he was not giving strong encouragement to the use of the gift. He left room for the Holy Spirit, however, to exercise His sovereign will in the matter. Men tend to go to extremes, and when a doctrine of the Word is misused many believers avoid it or oppose it. But if the Lord were to throw out every doctrine that men have misapplied or abused, we would have no Bible left.

We believe that the New Testament indicates it was the purpose of God to suspend the use of the miraculous gifts, at least in wholesale fashion, but not because they had been used in the wrong way. Until God suspended their use, men were to have freedom in exercising them.

The Brevity of the Gift

The thought here is not for us to arbitrarily shut the door on the use of miraculous gifts, but to show what God Himself says in connection with them in the New Testament. If God indicates that some gifts were temporary, we have no right to close our minds to that evidence. Neither does it mean that we believe God does not intervene in miraculous ways in human affairs today. His power does not diminish with time, but God does not always do the same thing in the same way.

In I Corinthians 13:13, Paul mentions three gifts—faith, hope, and love. Of the three, love is the only one that is endless. Faith will be turned into sight, and hope will become a reality. Thus faith and hope will end, but love never will.

All other gifts mentioned in Scripture are limited by time. This includes the three specific gifts mentioned in 13:8: ". . . whether there be prophecies, they shall fail; whether there be tongues, they shall cease; whether there be knowledge, it shall vanish away."

Prophecy was fragmentary in Paul's day. He said, "We prophesy in part." The Lord revealed one truth with present or future significance to one prophet and another truth to another prophet. But Paul said, "When that which is perfect is come, then that which is in part shall be done away." This was partially fulfilled when the Scriptures as we have them today were completed. Then that phase of prophecy which had to do with the foretelling of events was no longer needed. But another phase of prophecy —that of forthtelling, the giving out of God's message to bring conviction to men's hearts—continues in our day. But it will not be needed after the events recorded in Revelation 20.

The gift of knowledge also was to cease. Knowledge means "the understanding of revelation." However, our knowledge is fragmentary at the present time. Even the Old Testament prophets did not always understand what God caused them to write. But God gave others the gift of knowledge to understand and interpret these things. There is a time coming when the whole truth of Scripture will be revealed to us. Then the need for the gift of knowledge will cease. For us this will likely be at the second coming of Christ.

Tongues is the third gift, and it "shall cease." Paul indicated the place of tongues when he said, "When I was a child, I spake as a child, I understood as a child, I thought as a child: but when I became a man, I put away childish things." Here Paul is seeking to show that when a Christian comes to full maturity he no longer needs signs. Signs are for children or for those of little faith, but a mature Christian puts away childish things. Paul makes reference to this again in I Corinthians 14:20: "Brethren, be not children in understanding; howbeit in malice be ye children, but in understanding be men."

As far as evil is concerned, we should be as innocent as little children; but as far as knowledge is concerned, we should think as men.

Another line of Scriptural truth bearing on this general subject of miraculous gifts and pointing to their early termination in God's program in this age is found in the Ephesian letter. In Ephesians 2:20-22 the church is likened to a building with foundation and superstructure. The foundation, we are told, is composed of the apostles and prophets, Jesus Christ Himself being the chief cornerstone.

In the fourth chapter the gifts of evangelists, pastors, and teachers are added to the list, with the indication that these last gifts carry on through the whole Church Age; or to employ the figure of the building, they continue throughout the superstructure (Eph. 4:11-16). On the other hand, the gifts of apostles and prophets are limited to the foundation and would end when the foundation was laid.

It is in connection with the gift of apostleship that Paul links the miraculous gifts, for he says in II Corinthians 12:12: "The signs of an apostle were wrought among you in all patience, in signs, and wonders, and mighty deeds." This surely indicates that the miraculous gifts were to be expected as long as the apostolic gift lasted. It is logical to conclude that when the apostolic era closed the time of abounding miracles ceased.

We do not mean to imply that God ended all miracle working at the close of the apostolic era. If we understand the Scriptures correctly, however, He did not continue to use the miracle gifts in the same way as He had done during the time of the early church.

There have been only a few periods in this world's history that might be termed times of abounding miracles. The deliverance of Israel from Egypt and their journey to Canaan was one such time. Under the hand and leadership of Moses, Israel saw not merely a dozen miracles, but forty years of miracles. The ministries of Elijah and Elisha were also times of the multiplying of miracles.

The same is true for the days of our Lord and the apostles. It was an era of abounding miracles. Furthermore, on the basis of the Word of God, we believe that the tribulation period will again see the exercise of miracles and the miracle gifts.

This does not mean that God has not performed miracles since the close of the apostolic era. What we are saying is that God has not seen fit to endow believers with these miracle gifts to any appreciable degree since that time. God's Person never changes, but His program does.

The More Excellent Way

It is necessary for us in studying such a subject as the gifts of the Spirit to distinguish between gifts of a temporary nature and gifts of an eternal nature. It is equally important for us to remember that there is a distinct difference between the gifts of the Holy Spirit and the fruit of the Holy Spirit (Gal. 5:22-23). Gifts are given for the performance of certain services. These may be imitated by Satan or his agents at times, as was the case when the Egyptian sorcerers imitated some of Moses' miracles (Exod. 7:10-12).

The religions of heathenism furnish many examples of speaking in tongues, but one example will be sufficient. In his book *Primitive Culture,* Dr. Taylor describes a scene in the Sandwich Islands when the god Oro was supposed to give his teaching through a priest who "ceased to act or speak as a voluntary agent, but with his limbs convulsed . . . would roll on the ground, foaming at the mouth and reveal the will of the god in shrill cries and sounds violent and indistinct, which the attending priest duly interpreted to the people."

It is not necessary, however, to go outside the bounds of our own country to find a false religion claiming to have, among other gifts, the gift of tongues. Mormonism, the cult in question, has made this claim from its early days.

It is evident, then, that speaking in tongues is not always the result of the work of the Holy Spirit. Satan can imitate the gift so cleverly that many people have been and still are being deceived by him.

On the other hand, the fruit of the Holy Spirit (the qualities of righteousness which are the result of the presence of the Spirit of God in the Christian) cannot be imitated by Satan. Furthermore, we learn from I Corinthians 12:31 that love is the basis for the proper administration of the gifts of the Spirit.

The way of love is indeed the more excellent way. It guards, guides, and fills the heart so that the believer serves God in a manner consistent with the holiness and love of God. This love is defined in I Corinthians 13.

The Christian will respond in love to the constraining love of Christ and seek the gifts that will allow him to do the most for the Lord and His people (Rom. 12:1-8). At the same time, recognizing that spiritual gifts are distributed under the sovereign will of the Holy Spirit, the fully surrendered believer will be content to employ to the full whatever gift or gifts God chooses to give him.

The way of love is indeed the more excellent way.

4

THE USE
AND ABUSE
OF TONGUES
(Part 2)
by Theodore H. Epp and John I. Paton

There were at least sixteen spiritual gifts in the early church. They are listed in such passages as Romans 12, I Corinthians 12, 13, 14, and Ephesians 4:7-16. Some of these gifts are with us today; others, as the gift of apostleship, are not.

Gifts of the Spirit are not to be confused with the natural abilities of God's people, though, undoubtedly, there is a sanctifying and enriching work of the Holy Spirit with regard to such, making them of service to the Lord. Spiritual gifts are related to the new birth, while native gifts are related to the natural birth. The gifts named in the preceding Bible passages have their source in God (Rom. 12:3), are provided through Christ as the result of His triumphant resurrection and ascension (Eph. 4:7-16), and are distributed by the sovereign will of the Holy Spirit (I Cor. 12:8-11).

In the church at Corinth a great deal of interest and, sad to say, confusion also, centered in the gift of tongues. Apparently, there was something about this gift that caught the attention of the Corinthian believers, many of whom had been delivered from heathenism through the missionary work of the apostle Paul. The place they gave this gift caused the apostle, under the inspiration of the Holy Spirit, to deal with certain miracle gifts of the Spirit, showing the place the tongues-gift had in relation to them and correcting the abuses that had grown up in Corinth with respect to it.

Two books in the New Testament furnish the background for a study of this subject. One is the Book of Acts, a book of history, and the other is I Corinthians, a book of doctrine and moral instruction.

In the Book of Acts, three chapters contain specific information on the gift of tongues. The second chapter, dealing with the coming of the Holy Spirit at Pentecost, describes the initial appearance of the gift.

The second record is in chapter 10 where the Holy Spirit came upon new believers among the Gentiles, and they spoke in tongues. We know from Peter's words that the gift of tongues in the household of Cornelius was the same as on the Day of Pentecost. Peter said, as he related the event to the Jewish Christians in Jerusalem: "As I began to speak, the Holy Ghost fell on them, as on us at the beginning" (Acts 11:15).

The third occurrence is in Acts 19 where certain disciples of John were brought up-to-date by Paul on what God had done through the Lord Jesus and through the Holy Spirit. When Paul laid his hands upon these new believers in Christ, the Holy Spirit came upon them "and they spake with tongues and prophesied."

Tongues at Pentecost
(Acts 2)

We must first clearly understand the nature of the gift of tongues as revealed in this key chapter. At the time covered by the events here recorded, Jewish people were assembled in Jerusalem from many different countries of the world. The languages and dialects of those countries were foreign to the disciples, who were Galileans. Yet, when they were filled with the Spirit they "began to speak with other tongues" (2:4), and were understood by the visitors from these foreign lands.

The word "tongues" is the translation of the Greek word *glossa* whose primary meaning is the physical organ of speech and taste we call the tongue. A secondary meaning is "language." (Today the subject of tongues is often called "glossolalia.")

The context of any passage in which this word occurs will clearly indicate which meaning should be given it. For example, if someone exclaims: "I burned my tongue!" he refers to the tongue in his mouth. But when a person says, "I speak the native tongue," he does not mean the physical organ but the native language or mother tongue of the country in which he resides or is passing through.

In Acts 2:4 the words "speak with other tongues" mean that the disciples spoke languages strictly different from their native tongue. In verses 6 and 8 of Acts 2, a different Greek word for languages is used. It is the word *dialektos,* the word from which our English word *dialect* is derived. This means, then, that the disciples were divinely enabled to speak not only the different foreign languages spoken by the visitors to Jerusalem, but also the different dialects of these same languages. The Phrygians and Pamphylians both spoke Greek, but in different dialects. Even the dialect of Judea differed from that of Galilee (Acts 2:7, 9; Mark 14:70). The Greek word *dialektos* always means languages. It has no other meaning.

This tells us the nature of the gift of tongues. It was the Spirit-given ability to tell of the wonderful works of God (Acts 2:11) in a foreign language which was not known previously by the one speaking it. No interpreters were needed at Pentecost because the languages spoken were understood by those who heard them.

Purpose of Tongues

One result of this remarkable gift was to gain the attention of the multitude which then came together and heard Peter's stirring message concerning the Lord Jesus Christ. Another and more important result was that God provided a sign to the Jews through this miracle gift that He was doing a special work among them.

The law was given under remarkable manifestations of power at Sinai. So it is to be expected that the beginning of God's new work at Pentecost would also be attended with supernatural manifestations. Concerning this latter work, the writer to the Hebrews stated: "How shall we escape, if we neglect so great salvation; which at the first began to be spoken by the Lord, and was confirmed unto us by them that heard him; God also bearing them witness, both with signs and wonders, and with divers miracles, and gifts of the Holy Ghost, according to his own will?" (Heb. 2:3-4).

The miracles wrought by our Lord were evidential signs of credentials proving Him to be the Messiah. When John the Baptist wondered if the Lord Jesus were actually the Messiah, our Savior's answer was, "Go and shew John again those things which ye do hear and see: The blind receive their sight, and the lame walk, the lepers are cleansed, and the deaf hear, the dead are raised up, and the poor have the gospel preached to them" (Matt. 11:3-5).

This message was plain to many of the Israelites. They understood the significance of the sign-works of Christ better than their leaders did and said, "When Christ cometh, will he do more miracles than these which this man hath done?" (John 7:31).

Paul's ministry and message were confirmed through remarkable gifts. He wrote to the Romans: "For I will not dare to speak of any of those things which Christ hath not wrought by me, to make the Gentiles obedient, by word and deed, Through mighty signs and wonders, by the power of the Spirit of God; so that from Jerusalem, and round about unto Illyricum, I have fully preached the gospel of Christ" (Rom. 15:18-19).

It was a characteristic of the Jews that they looked for signs (I Cor. 1:22; Matt. 16:4; John 4:48). It was also, as we have seen, God's plan to confirm by special, evidential signs the gospel message and its messengers wherever He deemed it necessary. Every great forward step of the gospel in the Book of Acts is characterized by certain signs. At Pentecost the rushing, violent wind, the tongues like as of fire, and the speaking in tongues were God's stamp of approval, both on the messengers and on the message. The audience was primarily Jewish, so the sign-gifts were in keeping with His purpose.

When Peter went to the house of Cornelius, he took with him six Jewish brethren (Acts 10:23-24; 11:12). The gospel was taking a new step forward. Gentiles were going to turn to the Lord. The evidence of God's work in their hearts was confirmed by their speaking in tongues. This convinced Peter and the six Jewish brethren with him. It also silenced the criticism of the Jewish leaders in Jerusalem when they called Peter to account for going to the house of Cornelius (Acts 10:44, 48; 11:15-18). Peter referred to this matter again at the council in Jerusalem where he emphasized the fact that God had chosen him to present the gospel to the Gentiles and confirmed His divine work in the Gentile hearts by giving them the Holy Spirit (Acts 15:7-8).

The twelve disciples of John the Baptist who came to a saving knowledge of Christ through Paul's ministry in Ephesus spoke in tongues and prophesied when the Holy Spirit came on them (Acts 19:1-7). This manifestation of the Spirit's power constituted a sign to these men of Jewish background that Paul's message had its source in God.

It is one thing for God to offer evidential signs to prove the truth of His message; it is something else again when a Christian seeks for signs before he will believe God. One who does belongs in the category of a babe in Christ rather than in the place of a mature believer. Whether the sign sought is the gift of tongues or something else, the indication is that the person has a weak faith rather than a strong faith.

An example of this is found in John 20:24-25: "But Thomas, one of the twelve, called Didymus, was not with them when Jesus came. The other disciples therefore said unto him, We have seen the Lord. But he said unto them, Except I shall see in his hands the print of the nails, and put my finger into the print of the nails, and thrust my hand into his side, I will not believe." Now this man who was weak in faith demanded to see before he would believe. He was just like many of the Corinthians who apparently thought they must have the gift of tongues as evidence of their being filled with the Holy Spirit.

Now see what Jesus did about Thomas's unbelief: "And after eight days again his disciples were within, and Thomas with them: then came Jesus, the doors being shut, and stood in the midst, and said, Peace be unto you. Then saith he to Thomas, Reach hither thy finger, and behold my hands; and reach hither thy hand, and thrust it into my side: and be not faithless, but believing" (John 20:26-27).

Our Lord gave Thomas this evidence so that he would not be without faith. At the same time Jesus said, "Thomas, because thou hast seen me, thou hast believed: blessed are they that have not seen, and yet have believed" (John 20:29).

In I Corinthians 1:22 Paul said, "For the Jews require a sign." So we see that there are those who will not believe unless they can see.

We learn from Romans 4:20-22 that although Abraham could not see the fulfillment of the promise, he believed God. Then God counted it to him for righteousness. Abraham was strong in faith and did not require a sign.

The unbelieving Jews sought a sign; but Jesus said, "An evil and adulterous generation seeketh after a sign; and there shall no sign be given to it, but the sign of the prophet Jonas" (Matt. 12:39). There is a judicial sign spoken of in I Corinthians 14:21, but that will be considered later.

Christ promised that the Holy Spirit would come to dwell within each believer (John 14:16). Concerning the Spirit our Lord said, "If any man thirst [for power, for the filling of the Holy Spirit], let him come unto me, and drink. He that believeth on me, as the scripture hath said, out of his belly shall flow rivers of living water" (John 7:37-38).

God fills our lives with His Holy Spirit when we come to Him thirsting, when we drink, when we believe the promise concerning the Holy Spirit. We need no signs to know that we are filled. His Word tells us that if we believe, we are filled.

Often those who seek for a sign to assure themselves they are filled with the Holy Spirit, withdraw from the fellowship of other Christians who are willing to believe God's promise concerning the filling of the Spirit without a sign. Such sign-seeking Christians are usually very critical. They lack the fruit of the Spirit in their hearts which is love. Their very attitude indicates that they are not filled with the Holy Spirit. Faith does not require sight. Read Hebrews 11 and see how true this is.

It is noteworthy in examining these accounts of the speaking in tongues in the Book of Acts that not in one single instance did any of the persons involved seek for tongues. The gift was bestowed by the Holy Spirit without their asking for it.

Not All Spoke in Tongues

This further observation is also very significant. Speaking in tongues was not in evidence among the three thousand who received the Lord Jesus at the preaching of Peter at Pentecost, yet they had the assurance of receiving the Holy Spirit (Acts 2:38). Miracles were not absent, but they were of another nature, of a moral and spiritual kind.

This multitude accepted as leaders in this new faith men who had no standing as scholars or as religious leaders among the Jews.

These three thousand accepted the simple ordinances of baptism and the Lord's Supper in place of the elaborate ritual of the temple.

The Jew believed, on the basis of Old Testament promises, that the evidence of God's blessing on him lay in his being prospered economically. But these new converts gave up some of their wealth, sharing it with the less fortunate among them. They put their money into a common fund so that fellow believers need not suffer undue hardship.

Above all, this group had received as their Redeemer, One whom the leaders of their nation had rejected and had crucified because of envy.

A similar pattern followed in the wake of the gospel message wherever it went, according to the record in Acts. The change in believers' minds, their new viewpoints and values, their devotion to the Person and work of Christ finally led their opponents to say that the Christians had turned the world upside down. This was the evidence of the presence of the Holy Spirit and of His work in their hearts. Speaking in tongues is not mentioned in Acts save in these three instances to which we have given our attention.

There is a significant truth in Acts 4:31 with regard to the filling of the Holy Spirit. There we read: "And when they had prayed, the place was shaken where they were assembled together; and they were all filled with the Holy Ghost, and they spake the word of God with boldness." Here again, the truth is that the disciples were filled with the Holy Spirit. And being filled with the Holy Spirit they began to speak, but not with other tongues. They spoke "the word of God with boldness." This was a manifestation of the gift of prophecy which is not so much foretelling events, but the forthtelling or teaching of the Word of God.

In both chapters 2 and 4 of Acts, we read how God's people were filled with the Holy Spirit. According to Acts 2, the apostles spoke in languages they had not previously learned. In Acts 4, they were given boldness by the Spirit to tell out the Word of God.

According to Acts 13:9-11, the apostle Paul was filled with the Holy Spirit and spoke. But in this case he did not speak in tongues nor did he prophesy. He spoke words of judgment on a tool of Satan who called himself Bar-jesus (son of Jesus), or Elymas. Paul pronounced judgment upon this evil man, but the apostle had to be filled with the Spirit before he could do so.

In Acts 19:6, a passage previously dealt with, both tongues and the gift of prophecy are mentioned as evidences of the Spirit's presence.

There is no ground for concluding from these instances in the Book of Acts that the initial sign of a person's receiving the Holy Spirit or being baptized by the Holy Spirit was the ability to speak in tongues. The coming of the Holy Spirit upon men and women was manifested in a number of different ways. And in this record the gift of tongues does not hold a prominent place. The gift of prophecy far outweighs it, and so do other spiritual gifts.

Neither can it be proved from Acts that speaking in tongues and the gift of tongues are two distinct spiritual manifestations. They are actually different aspects of the same gift. The gift of tongues was the cause, the speaking in tongues was the effect. No one spoke in tongues who did not have the gift of tongues.

One final observation is in order with reference to the gift of tongues in the Book of Acts. Without a question, the most spectacular exhibition of that gift was seen on the Day of Pentecost (Acts 2). Yet when Peter stood up and gave his Spirit-inspired message, the speaking in tongues fell into the background and the exaltation of Jesus Christ came to the foreground. After showing the divine source of the tongues like as of fire, the sound of the wind, and of the speaking in tongues, Peter went on to give the message of life through Christ who was crucified, buried, and raised from the dead. Here was no exaltation of a gift of the Spirit. Here was no sharing of a spectacular experience.

Our Savior had declared before the Spirit came that when He did come, He would speak of Christ (John 16:13-15). This is demonstrated throughout the Book of Acts. It is not men. It is not gifts. It is not even the Spirit of God Himself who is prominent, but the Person of the Lord Jesus Christ. This should be the test of every believer's life and every aspect of His ministry. Whom do we exalt—self, the gift, or the Savior? What is the heart and core of our conversation? Our experience? Our gifts? Or is it Christ who has a Name above all other names? This is not a minor point; this is major. This is the program followed by the Spirit of God as He works in the hearts of men.

5

SPEAKING IN TONGUES
(Part 1)
by Richard W. De Haan

The phenomenon called "speaking in tongues" has aroused a great deal of interest in recent years. Secular newspapers and magazines have featured lengthy articles on this subject. Many educated people in old-line, staid, denominational churches unblushingly proclaim that they speak in tongues. This is quite surprising, because only a few years ago any person who claimed this so-called charismatic gift was looked upon as a wild-eyed fanatic. Usually, he would be thought of as one who attended a small church made up mostly of uneducated people from the lower classes of society, where services were highly emotional and quite empty of intellectual content. Much of this has changed, however, and the person who is not ready to immediately endorse "speaking in tongues" as a genuine sign from God makes himself quite unpopular in many circles.

Not all who speak in tongues are in agreement as to the precise nature of the gift. Some look upon it as a speech of ecstasy in a heavenly tongue, while others believe they use actual languages and dialects they have never learned, but which are in use here on earth. As we begin our study we recognize that a number of basic questions must be answered. Is the gift of tongues really a sign that one has received the Holy Spirit? Should everyone earnestly pray to receive it? Is it for us today? In order to answer these questions we turn first of all to the testimony of Dr. Luke, the man of God used to give us that great historical document, the Acts of the Apostles. He tells us of three occasions when people spoke in tongues, and describes them.

The First Occasion

The first instance is found in the second chapter of Acts. Luke tells us,

> *And they were all filled with the Holy Ghost, and began to speak with other tongues, as the Spirit gave them utterance.*
>
> *And there were dwelling at Jerusalem Jews, devout men, out of every nation under heaven.*
>
> *Now when this was noised abroad, the multitude came together, and were confounded, because every man heard them speak in his own language.*
>
> *And they were all amazed and marvelled, saying one to another, Behold, are not all these who speak Galilaeans?*
>
> *And how hear we every man in our own tongue wherein we were born?*
>
> *. . . we do hear them speak in our tongues the wonderful works of God.*
>
> *And they were all amazed, and were perplexed, saying one to another, What meaneth this?*
>
> *Others, mocking, said, These men are full of new wine (Acts: 4-8, 11-13).*

We call your attention to four pertinent points:

1. The speaking was on the part of the 120 disciples.
2. The people present were Jews.
3. Each understood the spoken words in his own dialect.
4. The "tongues-speaking" did not lead the people to repentance and faith.

The sound as of a rushing mighty wind, the tongues of fire, and this tongues-speaking only incited wonder, amazement, and confusion. The three thousand did not turn to Christ until after Peter had preached to them in the language common to them all. Notice, too, that after Peter had preached his sermon and the convicted listeners called out, "Men and brethren, what shall we do?"(2:37), Peter did not tell them to agonize or pray that they might receive the baptism of the Holy Spirit and the gift of tongues.

There is no indication that any of the three thousand who were converted that day spoke in tongues. It is obvious that the gift of tongues exercised on the Day of Pentecost was not used to preach the gospel. Verse 11 tells us they spoke "the wonderful works of God." They undoubtedly were praising the Lord in languages they had never learned.

A careful reading of these verses also indicates that the speaking in tongues was not in a heavenly or unknown language. Some Bible students have taught that the Holy Spirit here worked a twofold miracle, first enabling the disciples to speak in a spiritual or heavenly language, and then miraculously giving to each listener the ability to hear this language in his own native tongue. A careful examination of this passage does not bear out this contention. Verse 4 tells us they began "to speak with other tongues [plural], as the Spirit gave them utterance." The sixth verse declares that the multitude was confounded because "every man heard them speak in his own language [dialect]." This is repeated in verse 11. We conclude, therefore, that the disciples were speaking in more than one language, and each spoke as the Holy Spirit individually gifted him. They were not using some language of ecstasy.

The Bible does not give us all the details of this scene. It is possible that the disciples in unison praised God, and that they supernaturally used words from each language group of the assembled multitude so that every person present recognized these words. It is more likely, however, that the disciples separated from each other so that those who were from the various language areas gathered in small groups to listen to those believers who were speaking in their particular dialect. The speaking was miraculous. There was no miracle in the hearing. We would also like to point out that you can search the second chapter of Acts very carefully, and you will not be able to find any indication that the gift of tongues was to give evidence that these disciples had received the baptism of the Holy Spirit.

God gave three miraculous signs on this occasion: (1) the sound like a rushing mighty wind filling the place where they were sitting; (2) the strange tongues as of fire distributed upon them, sitting like a torch upon each head; and (3) the spontaneous utterances by the disciples in languages unknown to themselves but familiar to the hearers.

These three miracles were confirmatory signs from God. The sound like a rushing mighty wind was a sign of the powerful yet invisible work of the Holy Spirit, while the tongues "as of fire" signified the purifying work of the Spirit upon His witnesses, and the "speaking in tongues" was a token of the universality of that message which they were now as Spirit-empowered witnesses to proclaim.

The Second Occasion

The second instance of the gift of tongues is found in Acts 10,

> *While Peter yet spoke these words, the Holy Ghost fell on all them which heard the word.*
>
> *And they of the circumcision who believed were astonished, as many as came with Peter, because on the Gentiles also was poured out the gift of the Holy Ghost.*
>
> *For they heard them speak with tongues, and magnify God . . . (Acts 10:44-46).*

This event has sometimes been called the "Gentile Pentecost" because of its great similarity to that which took place in Jerusalem on that day when the Holy Spirit suddenly descended upon the small band of Jewish disciples. It is actually an extension of the significance of Pentecost for the salvation of the Gentiles. God suddenly took things out of Peter's hands by sending the Holy Spirit upon these believing Gentiles, causing them to speak in tongues just as the original disciples did on the Day of Pentecost. Thus God supernaturally confirmed His acceptance of these Gentiles so that Peter and his Jewish companions might not for one moment question the propriety of their inclusion in the church.

That this "speaking in tongues" was the same supernatural phenomenon as that of Pentecost is clearly indicated by Luke's choice of words. "Magnify God" *(megalunonton ton Theon)* in Acts 10:46 is synonymous with "speak . . . the wonderful works of God" *(lalounton to megaleia tou Theou)* in Acts 2:11. (In both cases the words *laleo* and *megas* are used, though in different forms.)

These Gentile believers suddenly broke forth in praise to God in dialects they had never learned, but which the Jewish messengers could understand. This striking reminder of how they had also spoken in languages unfamiliar to them at Pentecost was a sign that Cornelius and his friends were indeed accepted by God. A short time later when Peter was called upon to defend his action in baptizing these Gentiles, he asked, "What was I, that I could withstand God?" (Acts 11:17). The "tongues" of Acts 10:44-46 are obviously of the same nature and for the same purpose as those on the day of Pentecost.

The Third Occasion

The third and last instance of speaking in tongues as recorded in the Acts of the Apostles is found in chapter 19. Paul met twelve disciples at Ephesus. He immediately sensed that something was lacking in the spiritual experience of these men, and asked about their baptism. He learned that they had received John's baptism by a convert or a follower of John the Baptist after our Lord's resurrection and ascension into heaven. They were quite ignorant of the great significance of the cross, the empty tomb, and Pentecost. Luke gives us a brief synopsis of what took place when they met the apostle Paul.

> *Then said Paul, John verily baptized with the baptism of repentance, saying unto the people that they should believe on him who should come after him, that is, on Christ Jesus.*
>
> *When they heard this, they were baptized in the name of the Lord Jesus.*
>
> *And when Paul had laid his hands upon them, the Holy Ghost came on them, and they spoke with tongues, and prophesied.*
>
> *And all the men were about twelve (Acts 19:4-7).*

We do not have a full description of all that Paul declared to them as he explained the great redemptive facts in the life, death, resurrection, and ascension of Jesus Christ. When they understood the message of salvation, they received Christ and were baptized. With the laying on of apostolic hands they then received the gift of the Holy Spirit, spoke in tongues, and prophesied. The laying on of hands was certainly done before a group of assembled people. God enabled these twelve men to break forth in praise, using languages they had never known but which the listeners could understand. This was a public testimonial sign to the Jews that the message and baptism of John had been superseded by the gospel of God's grace and Christian baptism.

It certainly should be conceded by all that the gift of tongues was the same on the latter two occasions as that on the Day of Pentecost. Luke describes these scenes, using the same terms as he did when he pictured the events on the Day of Pentecost. In these two instances the people who turned to Christ spoke in languages they had never known, but which were understood by those in the listening audience. Again the miracle was in the speaking, not in the hearing.

The Book of Acts contains no other specific mention of tongues. In only one other place do we find the exercise of this gift implied. This is in chapter 8 where we have the story of Philip's ministry in Samaria. The Samaritans were a mixed race, partly Jewish, partly Gentile, and had a religion which was also a mixture of the true faith of the Old Testament and many of their own false ideas. They were avowed enemies of the Jews, and each despised the other. Philip worked many miracles and healings in Samaria, and perhaps the gift of tongues was here displayed. These miracles must certainly be looked upon as signs to the Jews, showing them that God was accepting the Samaritans as His people in this age on an equal basis with them. In no other place is there even an implication that people received the gift of tongues at the time of, or subsequent to, their salvation. In other accounts of conversion to Christ in the Acts of the Apostles (at least twenty specific instances are related, including individuals and large groups of people), not a word is said about anyone receiving the gift of tongues.

Tongues Not to Be Sought

Furthermore, not once are any of these converts exhorted to seek the baptism of the Holy Spirit with this attendant sign-gift. Only three times—at Pentecost, at the home of Cornelius, and in Ephesus when Paul met John's disciples—did speaking in tongues accompany salvation; and not once is tongues-speaking set forth as a mark of spiritual power. The Book of Acts certainly does not support the contention of those who say that the gift of tongues is a sign that one has received the Holy Spirit. The vast majority of those who turned to Christ did not exercise this gift, and no one ever agonized or pleaded for it. It is certainly a gross error to say that the disciples met in the upper room to tarry before the Lord that they might receive the gift of the Holy Spirit. The Lord simply told them they were to wait in the city of Jerusalem until they would be endued with power from on high. In obedience they waited, and while they waited they prayed. The Day of Pentecost was the Old Testament feast which arrived fifty days after the Feast of Firstfruits. That day would have come even if the disciples had not been watching and praying. It was on God's calendar. In fulfillment of Old Testament typology it marked the birthday of the church, and inaugurated the age of the Spirit.

The Day of Pentecost can never return. It is history. The Holy Spirit has been poured out, the church has been brought into existence, and the apostolic sign-gifts have long since become unnecessary.

Its Value and Limitations

Most Bible students agree that the speaking in tongues, as recorded by Luke in the Acts of the Apostles, was a miraculous utterance in real languages that were unknown to the speaker. A large percentage believe that the gift of tongues discussed by Paul in I Corinthians is to be sharply distinguished from the phenomenon reported by Luke. There is no unanimity of viewpoint concerning this question, neither among those who advocate tongues-speaking, nor among those who do not believe it is a valid gift today. Many contend that the gift of tongues in Acts was the miraculous ability to speak in a foreign language, but that at Corinth it was an ecstatic type of speech different from human languages. We have come to the conclusion that there is no basic difference between the tongues-gift as we find it in Acts and that discussed by Paul in his letter to the Corinthian church. We take the position that real languages are involved, and we will give our reasons for this as we proceed in our study.

In approaching Paul's discussion in I Corinthians, let us bear in mind that this church was the most difficult and unspiritual of all of those to which Paul wrote. It was divided into warring factions. Members brought lawsuits against one another which were fought out in the civil courts. Open immorality was tolerated by this church. Many of its members had real problems because they tended to fall back into some of their old idolatrous practices. The Lord's Supper was conducted in a disgraceful manner. Some members denied the reality of the bodily resurrection. These were some of the characteristics of the Corinthian church which placed such a premium on speaking in tongues.

Remember, too, that this letter is one of Paul's earliest Epistles, written when the miracles and healings described by Luke in Acts were still much in evidence. In this carnal church quite naturally there would be a great desire for the sensational. The believers therefore placed tongues as the highest and most desirable of all the spiritual gifts. In the Book of Acts the gift of tongues was exercised as an initial confirmatory sign, and nothing indicates that it remained in the lives of believers as a continuing faculty. In the church at Corinth, however, this miraculous gift has been made a part of the worship services. The excesses and abuses of speaking in tongues had become a serious problem in the Corinthian church, and Paul through this letter sought to set things right.

The first thing the apostle did was to show them that they were putting greater value upon this gift than they should. In I Corinthians 12, verses 8 through 11, he gives us a listing of the spiritual gifts, and places this gift last.

> *For to one is given, by the Spirit, the word of wisdom; to another, the word of knowledge by the same Spirit;*
>
> *To another, faith by the same Spirit; to another, the gifts of healing by the same Spirit;*
>
> *To another, the working of miracles; to another, prophecy; to another, discerning of spirits; to another, various kinds of tongues; to another, the interpretation of tongues.*
>
> *But all these worketh that one and the very same Spirit, dividing to every man severally as he will (I Cor. 12:8-11).*

Again in verse 28 of this chapter this gift is mentioned last.

> *And God hath set some in the church, first apostles, secondarily prophets, thirdly teachers; after that miracles, then gifts of healings, helps, governments, diversities of tongues.*

Chapter 12 closes with the words,

> *But covet earnestly the best gifts; and yet show I unto you a more excellent way.*

Since this is one of the least of the gifts, it is not to be coveted.

In chapter 14, precisely the same emphasis is given regarding the relative value of tongues.

> *Follow after charity [love], and desire spiritual gifts, but rather that ye may prophesy (v. 1).*

The apostle Paul points out that prophecy is far more valuable for edification than tongues, when he says in verse 5,

> *I would that ye all spoke with tongues, but rather that ye prophesied; for greater is he that prophesieth than he that speaketh with tongues, except he interpret, that the church may receive edifying.*

Referring to his own personal life, he again declares that tongues-speaking is not to be valued nearly so much as prophecy and teaching.

> *I thank my God, I speak with tongues more than ye all:*
> *Yet in the church I had rather speak five words with my understanding, that by my voice I might teach others also, than ten thousand words in an unknown tongue (I Cor. 4:18-19).*

It should be obvious to any person who reads these chapters that the gift of tongues was not one of the highest gifts, nor one that every Christian should earnestly seek.

Not Intended for All

Secondly, God did not desire that every person should possess the gift of tongues. After enumerating the various special spiritual gifts, Paul asks seven questions:

> *Are all apostles? Are all prophets? Are all teachers? Are all workers of miracles?*
> *Have all the gifts of healing? Do all speak with tongues? Do all interpret? (I Cor. 12:29-30).*

Paul expected a negative answer to these questions, as indicated in the Greek text by his use of a brief two-letter word with each question. God did not make every Christian an apostle or prophet or teacher. Nor did He give to every Christian the gift of tongues or the interpretation of tongues. This is so clearly expressed in these verses that no one should fail to see the point.

Never in the entire New Testament are we told that the baptism of the Holy Spirit must take place in conjunction with "tongues." Quite the contrary is indicated by the fact that every believer has been baptized into the Body of Christ, and yet not every believer has spoken in tongues. In I Corinthians 12:13 we read:

> *For by one Spirit were we all baptized into one body, whether we be Jews or Gentiles, whether we be bond or free; and have been all made to drink into one Spirit.*

Every Christian has been made a member of the Body of Christ, and every Christian has been made a partaker of the Holy Spirit, but not all have spoken in tongues. In Acts 2:38 Peter told the assembled multitudes:

> . . . *Repent, and be baptized, every one of you, in the name of Jesus Christ for the remission of sins, and ye shall receive the gift of the Holy Spirit.*

Three thousand people obeyed this call to repentance and faith. These same people received the gift of the Holy Spirit as Peter promised; namely, the Holy Spirit Himself. Yet those three thousand did not speak in tongues.

A careful reading of Acts indicates that God, even in apostolic days, did not desire that everyone should speak in tongues. In Acts 6:1-7 we have the appointment of seven deacons who were full of the Holy Spirit. We have no indication that any of them spoke in tongues. Acts 9:17-19, gives us a description of the restoration of Paul's sight, his filling with the Holy Spirit, and his baptism. There is absolutely no indication that Paul spoke in tongues on this occasion. Barnabas is described as "a good man, and full of the Holy Ghost and of faith" (Act 11:24). Yet we have no indication whatsoever that he spoke in tongues. The historical record in the Book of Acts indicates clearly that only a few spoke in tongues, and Paul in I Corinthians 12:30 positively declares that not all possess the gift of tongues.

The third observation as we read I Corinthians 14 is that the gift of tongues in Corinth, while of the same nature we encounter in the

Book of Acts, is nevertheless far inferior. On three occasions in Acts we read that people were enabled to speak in a language they had not learned, but it was always in a tongue or tongues the listeners could understand. In Corinth, however, an interpreter was often needed. From what Paul says in I Corinthians 14:2, it is clear that frequently the message spoken in tongues could be understoood by no one in the meeting, and no interpreter could be found. The speaker may have felt elevated in spirit as he spoke, but the things uttered were secret to those present and were therefore of no value:

> *For he that speaketh in an unknown tongue speaketh not unto men, but unto God; for no man understandeth him; howbeit, in the spirit he speaketh mysteries.*

In verse 4 Paul declares:

> *He that speaketh in an unknown tongue edifieth himself, but he that prophesieth edifieth the church.*

Prophecy in the early church was one of the special gifts of the apostolic period. It enabled the speaker, on occasions when the Holy Spirit moved upon him, to proclaim to the church by inspiration a message from God in language that could be understood by all. On the other hand, the person who spoke in tongues uninterpreted might gain personal benefit but would not help the church.

The only condition under which the gift of tongues had value almost equal to that of prophecy was if the person speaking in tongues possessed the gift of interpretation also. This dual ability was apparently rare. Verse 5 declares:

> *I would that ye all spake with tongues, but rather that ye prophesied: for greater is he that prophesieth than he that speaketh with tongues, except he interpret, that the church may receive edifying.*

Paul asks the Corinthian Christians how valuable his ministry would be if he came to them speaking only in uninterpreted tongues, without prophecy which comes from revelation, and doctrine which issues from supernaturally bestowed knowledge. He shows them that both in music and speech there is no communication if one cannot distinguish the sounds. Therefore he urges the one who speaks in tongues to pray for the ability to interpret. He then speaks hypothetically, as if he were exercising only the partial gift, namely, that of speaking in tongues without interpretation. If he by the Holy Spirit's direct influence upon his spirit should pray in a tongue he himself did not understand, his spirit might receive blessing, but his mind would be unfruitful, producing no value in the understanding of the listeners:

> For if I pray in an unknown tongue, my spirit prayeth, but my understanding is unfruitful [in the lives of those who are listeners] (I Cor. 14:14).

He desires to pray as the Holy Spirit moves upon him, but also in a comprehensible language so that others can be blessed:

> What is it, then? I will pray with the spirit, and I will pray with the understanding also; I will sing with the spirit, and I will sing with the understanding also (I Cor. 14:15).

One reason Paul desired so strongly to pray in language intelligible to everyone present is because "the unlearned" cannot join in or receive blessing through a prayer he does not understand:

> Else, when thou shalt bless with the spirit, how shall he that occupieth the room [place] of the unlearned say Amen at thy giving of thanks, seeing he understandeth not what thou sayest? (I Cor. 14:16).

Not to Be Despised

Though Paul placed relatively little value on "tongues," he nevertheless did not despise the gift.

> I thank my God, I speak with tongues more than ye all:
> Yet in the church I had rather speak five words with my understanding, that by my voice I might teach others also, than ten thousand words in an unknown tongue (I Cor. 14:18-19).

In spite of this clear declaration that he often spoke in tongues, we have no recorded instance of his use of this gift. He certainly made it clear that he never spoke in tongues in church services. Undoubtedly Paul exercised the gift as we find it in the Acts of the Apostles. What a wonderful "sign" Paul's gift of tongues would be as he traveled about on his missionary tour! He would proclaim the gospel to people in the Aramaic language, and then after they were saved he would break forth in praise and prayer using the native dialect of his listeners. People today who know more than one language will testify that they are moved most deeply when they hear the language of their childhood, and that prayers and praises in this tongue are especially meaningful. Therefore, this was an immediate and striking sign to these new believers, especially the Jews, of the genuineness of the salvation Paul preached.

In conclusion, remember that the tongues in Acts were real languages, and we have good reason to believe that the gift in Corinth was basically the same. It is also clear that the gift exercised in Corinth was not nearly so wonderful nor manifestly supernatural. In Acts everyone understood without an interpreter because the speakers miraculously spoke in languages the hearers knew. In Corinth the speaker usually was not understood by anyone present, and no one was able to interpret the utterances for the worshipers. Even when one could interpret, the effect would not be nearly so great as when the listeners could directly understand the speaker. They had no way of knowing that the interpreter was accurately reproducing the tongue being spoken.

It will help us if we bear in mind that Corinth was a great center for the pagan worship of Aphrodite, the goddess of love. Here, as well as in many other pagan temples, the immoral priestesses spoke in ecstatic tongues as they carried on their frenzied dances. They did not use known languages. Although, it is very unlikely that God's genuine gift of tongues would have been similar to this heathen manifestation, it is possible that some of that which passed for the "gift of tongues" in Corinth was more like this pagan display than the genuine gift.

In the light of all these facts, how important it is that we harken to God's Word. Let us not set high value upon those gifts which Paul so deliberately gives a place of small importance. And let us make certain that we do not make the same mistake as did these early Christians.

6

SPEAKING IN TONGUES
(Part 2)
by Richard W. De Haan

We are now ready to consider carefully I Corinthians 14:20-25. These six verses are usually looked upon as the most difficult to understand in Paul's discussion of tongues. They are actually the key that unlocks to us the proper understanding of the nature and significance of the gift of tongues. Beginning with verse 20 we read,

> *Brethren, be not children in understanding: howbeit, in malice be ye children, but in understanding be men.*

In these words Paul enjoined the Corinthian Christians to become more mature in their understanding. Quite literally he said, "Brethren, stop being children in intelligence, but in evil keep on being babies." Little children prefer the spectacular, amusing, and showy things, rather than those that are of more intrinsic value. In emphasizing tongues over prophecy, these believers were childishly naive and simple, like an infant who prefers a brightly colored rattle to an expensive and useful instrument. Therefore he tells them if they are going to act like infants, they should be like them in malice but not in understanding.

When we consider this statement in the light of all the other things we know about the Corinthian church, and realize that heathenism was especially strong in Corinth, we can understand why Paul wrote to these Christians about tongues in such a careful and guarded manner. These believers had a real problem in relation to paganism. Paul had to warn them strongly concerning the purchase of food that had been offered to idols. He found it necessary to specifically admonish against gross sexual sins, because heathenism was continuing to influence many of these weak and carnal believers. In Corinth a great temple had been erected in honor of the Greek goddess Aphrodite, which in Latin was called "Venus." The depraved worship of this pagan deity featured among other things ecstatic speaking in tongues.

The authentic gift of tongues was present in the Corinthian church, but unfortunately some of the people, sincerely believing they were exercising the heavenly gift, were actually in a state of hysteria, reproducing the frenzied type of tongues-speaking that prevailed in the heathen temples. Since they were sincere, though wrong and acting completely under the sway of their emotions, Paul wished to be very careful that he would not harm their weak faith. Instead of telling them their gift was not genuine if no one could interpret, he simply discouraged them, even forbade them, from exercising it in public. When he said they could practice tongues-speaking in private, he was not *recommending* it as a devotional exercise for individual worship. He wisely *suggested* this, knowing that in private they would do very little of it, for it was the childish yearning for recognition that was motivating many of them. They were not mature enough to hear the stark naked truth that a great deal of the practice they valued so highly was not really a gift from God.

The apostle Paul gently showed the Corinthian believers first of all that the gift of tongues is of less value than the other spiritual gifts; secondly, that not all are given this gift; and thirdly, that speaking in tongues without interpretation is of absolutely no value in the public services of the church. An understanding of these facts coupled with a proper Christian maturity would eliminate the problems this church faced concerning tongues.

An Old Mistake Repeated

The admonition to these Christians in Corinth brought to the mind of Paul a situation in Judah when the leaders, acting in a very childish manner, accused the prophet Isaiah of treating them like little children. In I Corinthians 14:21 the author is quoting from Isaiah 28, verses 11 and 12:

> *In the law it is written, With men of other tongues and other lips will I speak unto this people; and yet for all that will they not hear me, saith the Lord.*

The prophet was speaking to the court of Ahaz, king of Judah. To these men he first declared that God's judgment would soon fall upon the northern kingdom whose chief men at this moment were ignoring God, unmindful of the great calamity soon to befall them at the hands of Assyria. He pointed out that Israel's only hope is in God, but that these blind leaders will not turn to Him (Isa. 28:1-6). Having issued this warning concerning the fate of the northern kingdom, Isaiah then directed the attention of Ahaz and his cohorts to their own sinful condition. He described them in the filth of their drunkenness and moral depravity. They were behaving exactly like the doomed heads of Israel.

Verses 9 and 10 give us the scoffing reaction of these men to Isaiah's message. He had denounced their evil and proclaimed the certainty of judgment, but they were extremely resentful of his clear and simple message. I would like to paraphrase their mocking reply, "Who does Isaiah think he is talking to? Babies who have just been weaned? He keeps on preaching the same old thing—rule upon rule, line upon line, the monotonously simple refrain that God is going to punish us if we keep on sinning. We are getting tired of this simple Sunday school moralizing."

In verse II we have God's answer to their scornful words. Our King James Version begins this verse with the conjunction "for." It should begin with the adversative "but." Let me again paraphase these words so that you will get them clearly in your mind. "But you will not always hear this simple message that you despise. With the lips of foreigners whose speech will sound like stammering to you, I am going to speak to you in the future when you go into captivity. You have refused the simple and understandable message of my prophet. Therefore, when you are taken captive and live in the presence of *languages you do not understand,* I am going to drive home to you in judgment the truth you have rejected, until finally your haughty pride is broken" (Isa. 28:11-13).

Paul quotes this passage from Isaiah to show these Corinthian believers that by their failure to appreciate the simple language of prophecy they were making the same mistake the men of Judah did. In that respect these weak Christians in Corinth were like the scornful leaders in Judah. Paul therefore draws this conclusion,

> *Wherefore, tongues are for a sign, not to them that*
> *believe, but to them that believe not; but prophesying serveth*
> *not for them that believe not, but for them which believe*
> *(I Cor. 14:22).*

It was unbelief on the part of the leaders of Judah, a childish refusal
to heed the simple words of prophetic warning, that made it
necessary for God to speak to them in the foreign tongues of their
captors. Mature people appreciate straighforward and truthful
speech rather than ambiguous and meaningless oracles which may
sound very mysterious and exciting. Thus both the men of Judah
and the Corinthian believers were behaving like children. Tongues
were a sign to them in their unbelief. For the people of Judah and
Israel the tongues of their captors did not lead them back to God.
They became a sign of judgment rather than salvation. Relating
this to the Corinthian Christians, we must remember that the word
Paul used here, and which is translated "believe not," has a
general meaning that can be applied to the utter lack of faith which
marks an unbeliever, or the relative lack that can mar a Christian's
life. It is the same word the Lord Jesus used when He said to
Thomas, ". . . be not faithless, but believing" (John 20:27).

"Tongues" is therefore a sign to promote faith in those who have
a lack. This was the purpose of the tongues of foreigners by which
God spoke to the children of Israel and Judah, and this was the
purpose of "tongues" in Corinth. These weak Christians in
Corinth were granted an exercise of the gift of tongues in order that
their faith might be strengthened. There is no indication that God
gave the gift of tongues to any of the other churches. Apparently
they did not need it. The carnality and immaturity of the Corinthian
Christians were such that seemingly they could not receive help
through the simple and straightforward message of prophecy.
They felt the need for something spectacular, something outward
and evident. In the gift of tongues God simply stooped to meet the
special need of these babes in Christ.

This quotation from Isaiah clinches our contention that the gift
of tongues exercised in Corinth involved the use of actual
languages just as it did in the Acts account. Remember that Paul

and Luke use identical terms in discussing this gift. Furthermore, the foreign tongues to which the people of Israel and Judah were exposed during their captivity were real languages. In speaking of them the apostle Paul uses the Greek word *heteroglossois*, the same word with which he depicted the special, miraculous, charismatic gift of tongues. This certainly strengthens our conviction that the gift of tongues was never a speech of ecstasy in a "new" language.

In heathen religions there has always been a great deal of tongues-speaking. Since the gift of tongues was a "sign" in every instance of its occurrence in the Book of Acts, and it is declared in I Corinthians 14:22 to be a sign to them that believe not, we certainly must insist that all genuine uses of the gift were in real languages. Anything other than this could not have been a sign to the Jewish people. It would have looked to them like a carbon copy of that which was taking place in heathen temples.

Paul went on to point out also that a service marked by tongues-speaking would not lead unsaved people to Jesus Christ.

> *If, therefore, the whole church be come together into one place, and all speak with tongues, and there come in those that are unlearned, or unbelievers, will they not say that ye are mad?*
>
> *But if all prophesy, and there come in one that believeth not, or one unlearned, he is convicted of all, he is judged of all.*
>
> *And thus are the secrets of his heart made manifest; and so falling down on his face he will worship God, and report that God is in you of a truth (I Cor. 14:23-25).*

If an earnest inquirer and an unbeliever came into a service where all were speaking with tongues they would simply conclude that the people were mad. Remember that on the Day of Pentecost the speaking in tongues, along with the sound of the mighty rushing wind, helped draw the multitude. This was undoubtedly a sign to the bewildered believers, indicating to them the universal extension of the gospel to people of every language. These signs, however, did not have a very desirable effect upon the unsaved. It puzzled them to the extent that some said, "What meaneth this?"

and led others to say, "These men are filled with new wine." No one turned to Christ until Peter preached his great sermon. He did not preach in tongues, but used the universal language of his day which everybody could understand. Peter was exercising the gift of prophecy, divinely inspired speech in a common language of the people, and his message led three thousand to confess Jesus Christ as their Savior. Thus prophecy, not tongues, in the church in Corinth would reveal to those who came into the assembly from the outside their lost condition before God, and would draw them to Christ.

I realize that many sincere Christians may be offended by some of these statements. This grieves my heart, since my motivation in bringing these studies has been to present the teaching of God's Word faithfully and honestly. I have no rancor or bitterness in my heart toward those who may differ with me. So please accept this teaching in the spirit in which it is given. If some of these things have been shocking or new to you, do not become upset and angry; instead, please reread this message with an open Bible before you. Check out what I have said with the Word of God and let that be your guide.

Its Regulation and Final Cessation

In this last section on "tongues" we will center our attention upon I Corinthians 14:26-40 where the apostle Paul lays down a number of regulations for the conduct of the church service in Corinth. But first let me summarize some definite conclusions we have reached through our study thus far.

1. The gift of tongues as described in Acts and discussed in I Corinthians 12 and 14 was the supernatural ability to speak in a *real* language, previously unknown to the speaker but understood by the hearers.

2. Tongues-speaking was a sign to confirm the gospel message in the apostolic age. In each of its three occurrences in Acts it was a confirmatory sign. It was not repeated. In each case it was a special sign to the Jews concerning the universal nature of the gospel.

3. The gift of tongues as it was exercised in Corinth was also a sign, not for the winning of converts, nor as a token of the

reception of the Holy Spirit, but to strengthen the faith of weak and carnal believers. There is no evidence that it existed in any other apostolic churches, because apparently they did not need it.

4. The practice of tongues-speaking in Corinth had become a real problem. Some were imitating the kind of "tongues" that was common in the heathen worship rituals, and there was a general and unwholesome emphasis upon this gift among these carnal Corinthian believers.

We must remember that the genuine gift of tongues as we saw it in the Book of Acts had not yet been completely withdrawn. Therefore, all the tongues-speaking was not false or evil. Paul knew, however, that this heathen practice had made some inroads into the Corinthian church, and definitely wished to correct the situation. He did not want to shake the faith of those who on some occasions exercised the genuine gift of tongues, and therefore he did not berate them nor bluntly tell them that a false element had entered in, and that some of them were unwittingly deceiving themselves. Rather, he laid down a number of positive regulations and principles which would enable these Christians to distinguish between the proper and improper use of the gift.

1. He showed them that "tongues" was the least important of all the gifts. In I Corinthians 12, verses 10 and 28, he lists it last.

2. He emphasized that "prophecy" is far superior to "tongues" (I Cor. 14:1-5).

3. He made it very clear to these Corinthian Christians that God did not intend for all to speak in tongues. The seven questions he asked in I Corinthians 12:29-30, clearly demand a negative answer.

4. Paul pointed out that uninterpreted "tongues" was completely worthless in an assembly (I Cor. 14:5-19).

5. In I Corinthians 14:20-22, he established again that the sign of tongues was given in Corinth to bolster the faith of weak and immature believers.

6. In I Corinthians 14:23-25, he points out that the exercise of

tongues in a public meeting would repel the unsaved rather than contribute to their salvation.

Having clearly established these things, Paul now discusses the proper regulation of the gifts of tongues and prophecy in the public services of the assembly. Turning to verse 26, we read,

> *How is it, then, brethren? When ye come together, everyone of you hath a psalm, hath a doctrine, hath a tongue, hath a revelation, hath an interpretation. Let all things be done unto edifying.*

This verse clearly indicates that the public services in the Corinthian church were very informal, and that a number of people participated in the speaking. Such a situation leads to excesses unless some careful regulations are observed. For that reason we read in verses 27 and 28,

> *If any man speak in an unknown tongue, let it be by two, or at the most by three, and that by course; and let one interpret.*
>
> *But if there be no interpreter, let him keep silence in the church; and let him speak to himself, and to God.*

One, two, or three were to exercise "tongues" in a service. This was to be done in turns, and only when the words could be immediately interpreted. By telling a believer to use the gift in private if no one present could interpret, Paul was not *recommending* "tongues" as a vehicle in personal devotions. He knew that those who were sincerely, but mistakenly, exercising what they thought to be the gift of tongues would soon see their error if they practiced it privately. Others would naturally lose interest, for it was the thrill of public display that motivated many of them to place such a high value upon speaking in ecstasy.

Women and Tongues?

The command of verses 34 and 35 in I Corinthians 14 has been the subject of much discussion. Here it is:

> *Let your women keep silence in the churches: for it is not permitted unto them to speak; but they are commanded to be under obedience, as also saith the law.*
>
> *And if they will learn anything, let them ask their husbands*

at home: for it is a shame for women to speak in the church.

Paul was not demanding absolute silence on the part of women. We know from other Scripture portions that women sometimes participated in this way. Acts 21:9, tells us that Philip had four daughters who prophesied. Moreover, in I Corinthians 11:3-10, Paul had given instructions about how the women were to dress when they prayed or when they prophesied in the church. Paul certainly wouldn't contradict what he had just written.

In view of this, we believe that the prohibition here has a direct relation to the problems of this chapter; namely, the exercise of the gift of tongues. Women were not to speak in tongues, not to publicly ask questions that would arise in connection with them. It is obvious that the "tongues" part of the church meetings had become highly emotional, and that it led the women to behave in a very unbecoming manner. An outsider might have concluded that their conduct was similar to that which took place in the heathen temples, where the prostitutes and other immoral women in their frenzied dervishes would often speak in such tongues. Therefore, it was a shame for women to speak in such services, and we concur that the hysterical behavior of women in many present-day "tongues" meetings is a disgrace. If all Pentecostal groups today would enforce this rule, not permitting women to participate in tongues services, it would do a great deal to bring about the end of the movement.

In verse 36 Paul asks the Corinthian Christians what makes them think they can conduct themselves in a manner different from the other churches,

> *What? Came the word of God out from you? Or came it unto you only?*

This confirms our previous statement that the situation in Corinth was unique, other churches not having experienced the same problem.

Paul's final exhortation in this fourteenth chapter is found in the last two verses, 39-40:

> *Wherefore, brethren, covet to prophesy, and forbid not to speak with tongues.*
>
> *Let all things be done decently and in order.*

The leaders at Corinth were instructed not to forbid "tongues," because God had graciously given this gift to that weak church. They were explicitly to obey the directions he had laid down, however, and all things were to be done decently and in order. The apostle Paul would not have been very favorably impressed by a service in which men and women with wild-eyed frenzy and hysteria either pray for or speak in tongues.

If the Corinthian church took seriously Paul's estimate of "tongues," placed the emphasis upon the better gifts, and carefully followed his regulations, we can be certain that not only did their problems in connection with "tongues" services come to an end, but the whole matter of speaking in tongues disappeared. Paul's second letter to this church does not touch upon the subject. It was no longer a problem. "Tongues" had ceased.

The gift of tongues was never intended to be a permanent feature of the church. It is one of the temporary charismatic gifts which served a special function during the transitional period while the church gradually lost its Jewish character, and the New Testament was in the process of being written. Apostleship ended with the death of John. Prophecy (inspired utterances directly from God) ended with the completion of the New Testament. The gifts of miracles and healings were gradually withdrawn, so that in Paul's later epistles we find that he no longer exercised these powers. The gift of "tongues" likewise was intended by God only as a temporary sign. This gift, in a less striking form than that seen in Acts, was given by God to the Corinthian Christians to help them in their weak, childish, immature faith. They lusted for the sensational display gifts even as the children of Israel lusted for meat in the wilderness. Psalm 106:15 is perfectly applicable to their situation:

> *And he gave them their request, but sent leanness into their soul.*

The gift for which they clamored God gave them, seemingly with reluctance, but it became the source of confusion and difficulty in their services.

We believe that people today who claim for themselves the New Testament gift of tongues are mistaken, even though many testify that speaking in tongues has been a great blessing in their lives. We do not question the sincerity of these Christian people, nor would we ridicule them. We must insist, however, in love, that the exercise of so-called tongues-speaking has brought much confusion and harm to the church. Congregations have been torn apart through problems arising out of it. Some people who practice "tongues" have a tendency to look upon others who do not as being inferior Christians. Many sincere believers, earnestly wanting God's best, but not possessing the emotional make-up for this kind of experience, have made themselves wretched in their efforts to speak in tongues.

Not only does this practice cause division and spiritual frustration, it also has led some into gross carnality. Tongues-speaking is a common phenomenon in heathenism, and this state of excitement opens the door to strange excesses. Among some present-day tongues groups, the assembled people do not conduct themselves in a decent and orderly manner.

It is tragic, yet true, that a person may sincerely believe he is exercising a genuine gift from God, while in actuality he is playing a trick on himself.

The Bible does not give us any reason to expect a repetition of the events that occurred on the Day of Pentecost. For that reason, we would encourage all who desire to know and to do God's will to turn away from the voices of emotional experience and feelings and direct their attention to the Word of God. Whereas the Bible nowhere urges you to seek the gift of tongues, God does strongly call upon you and me to manifest and develop the spiritual graces of Galatians 5:22-23:

> . . . *love, joy, peace, longsuffering, gentleness, goodness, faith,*
> *Meekness, temperance [self-control].* . . .

7

IS THE CHARISMATIC MOVEMENT OF GOD?
by Dick Meier

The modern-day tongues movement is a dangerous, religious fraud that is bringing much confusion, division, and diversion among God's people. I do not accept the validity of the modern tongues movement for at least five reasons.

I
It is not the same phenomenon as that of the New Testament era.

What was the gift of tongues in the New Testament era? It was the supernatural ability to articulate speech in a previously unlearned language. "And how hear we every man in our own tongue, wherein we were born?" (Acts 2:8).

Those who seek to promote the tongues movement today emphasize their "unknown tongues." However, in every case without exception the gift of tongues in the New Testament involved an intelligible foreign language. The word "unknown" as it appears in I Corinthians 14 in the King James Version of the Bibe is in italics. It was added by the English translators, but it was not in the original. When Paul talked about the gift of being used "without understanding," as in I Corinthians 14:2 and 14, he was simply saying, "in exercising this gift as opposed to the gift of prophecy, you need to have an interpreter. Your understanding of a spiritual truth, if communicated in a foreign language without an interpreter, will not be fruitful or beneficial to those who may hear you."

Tongues-speaking was not an unintelligible babbling for the sake of an experience based upon emotion and feeling. Its original purpose according to Acts 2 was to communicate the gospel of the

Lord Jesus Christ. According to I Corinthians 14:22 it was a special "sign" gift to help unbelieving Jews to believe the gospel or to believe that the gospel had been given to the Gentiles as well as to the Jews. In I Corinthians 13:1 when Paul speaks about the tongues of angels, he is using this phrase as an illustration of contrast in the same manner as he uses the extreme of giving his body to be burned. He is not defining the gift of tongues.

Is the gift of tongues in the church today? No! Some spiritual gifts were temporary in nature, having been prominent in the days of the apostles (Heb. 2:3-4). Other spiritual gifts were to be permanent and are here today. Among the temporary gifts was the gift of tongues (I Cor. 13:8). These special "sign" gifts were given to the apostles to demonstrate that they were accredited by God (Mark 16:20). With the completion of the New Testament and its almost universal acceptance by those true to God, the need for further display of miraculous works ceased.

The preacher of today does not need the outward evidence or ability to heal or to speak with tongues to substantiate the validity of the gospel. Rather, the written Word speaks for itself and it is attended by the convicting power of the Holy Spirit. The temporary gifts were much like scaffolding that is erected when a new building is being built. Once the construction is finished, the scaffolding is removed; it is no longer required.

As Paul was writing to the Corinthians, as is indicated by I Corinthians 13:9, the New Testament had not yet been completed. Their knowledge of God's will was only in part and their resources for preaching the Word were still incomplete.

Notice verse 10: "But when that which is perfect is come, then that which is in part shall be done away." This, no doubt, is referring to the time when the New Testament would be completed and accepted by the early church. "That which is perfect" does not refer to Jesus. The word "that" is in the neuter gender which refers to an inanimate object and the word "perfect" is better translated "completed." "When that which is completed is come [referring to the completed Word of God], then that which is in part [that is, the temporary gifts, the scaffolding] shall be done away."

Once the completed revelation of God's Word would be given, read, and understood, it would be as complete for knowing God's will as speaking to Jesus Christ face to face instead of merely "seeing through a glass darkly." In fact, Peter even speaks of the written Word as something "more sure" than seeing face to face as he had on the Mount of Transfiguration (II Peter 1:16-19).

How can we account for the experience of many fine people? Shall we allow anyone's interpretation of his experience make the Word of God of noneffect? Who is the final judge—a person's analysis of an experience or the Word of God? I will believe the Word of God and look for some other meaning behind a person's experience.

Is the increasing numbers of people involved in this movement a sign that it is of God? If one answers Yes, then that logic should also be applied to the growing cults. The answer is obviously, No.

II
Its claim that "tongues" is the evidence of the baptism in the spirit is based upon ignorance of the Scriptures.

The very foundation of the modern-day tongues movement is its claim that "tongues-speaking is the initial evidence of the baptism in the Holy Spirit."

First of all, let us categorize our terminology. The "indwelling of the Holy Spirit" is a ministry which takes place the moment of the believer's regeneration (Cor. 6:19; Rom. 8-9).

Another ministry of the Holy Spirit which automatically takes place at the same time is the "baptism *by* the Holy Spirit" (I Cor. 12:13). This is that act whereby the believer is incorporated into the Body of Christ. It is the union of the believer with Christ. Since all true believers are in Christ, this baptism "by means of " (instrumental case—"by the agency of ") the Holy Spirit, takes place also at the instant of regeneration.

The third ministry of the Holy Spirit is the "infilling" of the believer by the Holy Spirit. Paul illustrates this ministry by a contrast in Ephesians 5:18: "Be not drunk with wine, wherein is excess, but be filled with the Spirit." As the drunkard is under the control of something other than himself, so the Christian should be under the *control* of the Holy Spirit. The Holy Spirit indwells, but the believer is to yield over every department of his life, moment by moment, to the indwelling Holy Spirit. There are times when the believer is filled with the Spirit and times when the believer may not be filled with the Holy Spirit depending upon his yieldedness.

This third ministry is synonymous with the "baptism *in* the Holy Spirit." In Acts 1:5, before the Lord Jesus ascended, He told the disciples that not many days hence they would be baptized with (*in*) the Holy Ghost. This King James English word "with" is the Greek preposition *en* used in the locative sense showing the location or sphere into which the baptized ones shall be baptized. It should be translated as "ye shall be baptized *in the sphere of* the ministries and power of the Holy Spirit."

In the Greek language the definite article related to our word "the" *identifies* its proper noun. But when there is an absence of the definite article, the emphasis is upon the *qualities* or *ministries* of the proper noun. For instance, the famous verse on the Holy Spirit in Luke 11:13 is not a suggestion to pray for the Person of the Holy Spirit to come into the life of the believer, but rather a suggestion that the believer keep on asking for the ministries and power of the Holy Spirit in his life. This is precisely the effect of the infilling ministry of the Holy Spirit.

In Acts 2 when the days had been fulfilled and the Day of Pentecost had fully come, the ministry of the Holy Spirit that took place upon the believers gathered there is here described as the "filling" ministry of the Holy Spirit according to verse 4. Thus Jesus' description and then Luke's description under the inspiration of the Holy Spirit make the "baptism into the sphere of the power and ministries of the Holy Spirit" synonymous with being "filled with the Holy Spirit." This wonderful, empowering ministry by the Holy Spirit that would not only be available to kings and prophets, but also to the common believers and their sons and daughters, young men, old men, servants, and even handmaidens, was that which was often referred to by John the Baptist in his ministry.

We object when people interpret our rejection of modern-day tongues as a rejection of the supernatural work of the Holy Spirit. We depend upon His work. His work is wonderful and miraculous, but always consistent with His Book rightly divided.

When people talk to me about the baptism of the Holy Spirit, I try to pin them down to a discussion either of the baptism *by* the Holy Spirit into the Body of Christ, or the baptism by the *Lord Jesus Christ* into the sphere of the power of the Holy Spirit, which is the same thing as being "filled with the Holy Spirit." I often draw a diagram which illustrates the difference between the baptizer, the baptized one, and the sphere into which he is being baptized.

John the Baptist baptized his converts into the sphere of water. At regeneration the Holy Spirit, who is the agent, baptizes the believer into the sphere of the Body of Christ. But Jesus pointed the eyes of the disciples toward the Day of Pentecost and promised that He would be the baptizer and that He would baptize them into the sphere of the power and ministries of the Holy Spirit.

Why do some claim that tongues is the initial evidence of the baptism in the Holy Spirit? First, Jesus never said that "tongues" would be the sign but rather *power for witnessing* (Acts 1:8).

Second, the prophet Joel never said that "tongues" would be the evidence. It was Joel who was quoted by Peter when he described what was happening on the Day of Pentecost. Joel claimed that the evidence of that day would be prophecy. There are two words in the original for "prophecy." One is *propheteuo* which means "to preach and teach God's Word." The second is *prophemi* which means "to foretell events." The second word is not used by Joel, but rather the first, which means that the evidence is simply that people will have a burden to preach and teach God's Word and try to get people saved.

Thirdly, "tongues" was only one of the many gifts of the Holy Spirit in the early days of the New Testament. Paul asked a question in I Corinthians 12:30: "Do all speak with tongues?" As he asked this question, he was expecting a No answer. In the Greek, when a question such as this is asked, there is a little word placed before the question which shows which answer the author wanted from his readers. If he wanted a Yes, there would be the two letters *ou*. If he wanted a No, there would be the two letters *ma*. As Paul asked this question, he used *ma*. Therefore, if all do not speak with "tongues," the "tongues" gift even then could not possibly have been the evidence of the baptism in the Spirit.

Also, some of the 120 in Acts 2 did not then have "the evidence" of the fullness of the Holy Spirit. Some of them did not speak in a foreign language, even on that occasion. The disciples spoke the language of the people of Galilee, which was Aramaic. Some of the foreign Jews present on the day of Pentecost were from the area of Judea (v. 9). The Judeans at that time also spoke in Aramaic. All of the 120 were filled with the Spirit and all of them spoke out for God and witnessed for Christ, but there were some from Judea who heard in their own language which was Aramaic; thus some of the witnesses who naturally spoke Aramaic did not have their language changed in any way, only empowered. For instance, I could talk to a man from Canada, but I would not use a foreign tongue. Most Canadians speak English. The point would not be the language I was speaking but the subject we were talking about.

Lastly, the greatest soul-winners in later history have not spoken in "tongues." Go down the list: D. L. Moody, R. A. Torrey, Charles Finney, Billy Sunday, John R. Rice, the Bob Joneses, Bill Dowell, Jack Hyles, Tom Malone, Lee Roberson, Bob Gray, Bob Moore, Jerry Falwell, and others. The testimony is unanimous. Would someone dare to say that these men had not been filled with the Holy Spirit?

III
It strangely deemphasizes
the saving element of
the gospel of Christ.

The constant emphasis of the modern-day tongues movement is, "What is the Holy Spirit doing in you? How do you feel: What do you experience?" However, the emphasis of the New Testament believers was, "We preach not ourselves, but Christ Jesus, the Lord" (II Cor. 4:5). Their emphasis was not what they were experiencing, but rather what Jesus experienced for them at the cross. Paul said in I Corinthians 2:2: "For I am determined not to know any thing among you, save Jesus Christ, and him crucified."

The basics of the redemptive work of God for us are twofold: (1) what God has done for us in Christ at the cross, and (2) what God is doing in us by the Holy Spirit.

Number one is the gospel that saved (I Cor. 14:1-4); number two is the fruit of the gospel. Number one was accomplished outside of us at the cross; number two is being done in us day by day by the Spirit. Number one was perfect and complete; number two is imperfect and has its ups and downs. Our salvation rests on number one, not on number two. However, as you search the writings of those who promote the modern tongues movement you will find a strange vacuum concerning number one. Very little is ever said about the cross, about the finished work of Jesus Christ, about God's grace extended to us because of the shed blood, about God accepting us as His children because of Christ, not because of what is going on in our hearts, even in the name of the Holy Spirit.

Could it be that many who talk about inward experiences have never understood the meaning of number one which is the gospel? Could it be many claim to have the experience of "tongues" but have never had the experience of the new birth or have never seen the simplicity of salvation by grace?

IV
It is producing an unscriptural ecumenicity between believers and unbelievers.

It is easy to find statements in such magazines as *Christian Life* and other religious periodicals and newspapers that indicate that the tongues movement is overlapping many denominations. The thing that ought to awaken our good judgment is that many who are dedicated Catholics and who still believe in the idolatrous sacrifice of the mass and depend upon the second part of the redemptive work without the first as a basis of their salvation, as well as modernists who reject the virgin birth of Christ and the deity of Christ, are claiming this gift of "tongues."

How can these who are not really born again have the Holy Spirit living in their bodies when the Holy Spirit dwells only in the bodies of believers? Could it be that the spirit that is working in them is not the Holy Spirit, but is some other spirit? This so-called experience that many from this wide range of doctrinal positions are sharing is becoming their basis for fellowship. However, the Scripture places a completely different standard for the basis for fellowship. Second John 10 plainly says, "If there come any unto you, and bring not this doctrine [the doctrine of Christ], receive him not into your house, neither bid him God speed." The doctrine of Christ involves His eternal deity, His virgin birth, His sinless life, His substitutionary death, His bodily resurrection, salvation by grace through faith in Him, and also His words and views concerning the Scriptures.

I believe that there is a possibility that the tongues movement as it is being used today, could become a catalyst for the future ecumenical church under the Antichrist during the tribulation years just ahead after the Rapture takes place. It is interesting to note that Revelation 17 says that the ecumenical church during the tribulation will be under the direction of Rome and will draw its people together by signs and wonders produced by the false prophet (Rev. 17:11-14).

V
It sadly misuses a neglected Bible doctrine—the fullness of the Spirit.

It seems that the modern promoters of the tongues movement are concerned mainly for feelings. "How do you feel?" they ask. However, our concern for today should be not for feelings but for usefulness. Souls all around us are plunging into hell. Not very many people are standing in the gap to point men to the cross of Jesus Christ. Many people who should be busy winning souls to Jesus Christ are gathered together in small circles trying to arouse certain emotional feelings when they ought to be praying for power to win souls to Jesus Christ. Whenever the Bible talks about being filled with the Spirit, it emphasizes power for service, power for witnessing, power for soul winning (Luke 1:15; Acts 1:8; 4:29-33; 9:17-20; and 11:24).

We had to remove a missionary couple from the missionary support of our church when they explained to me that they had become involved in the tongues movement. They mentioned that their energies on the field had been redirected from winning souls to teaching Christians how to speak in "tongues." This is a typical pattern which seems to find its duplications in the lives of so many people who become involved in this false movement. They become preoccupied with childish toys and steered away from the greatest task a human being could ever do—that is to witness to lost sinners about Christ. Satan must rejoice when he sees soldiers leaving their guns, leaving the battle, to go back to the sidelines to play marbles with each other!

Satan is the great counterfeiter. The modern-day tongues movement, in my estimation, is being used by Satan to bring confusion, division, and diversion. Let us repent if we have been caught in such a snare.

8

TESTS FOR
THE TONGUES
MOVEMENT
by Harold Lindsell

The charismatic movement, sometimes called neo-Pentecostalism, is now a worldwide phenomenon. It has gained many adherents in the old-line Protestant denominations. It has also made broad inroads into Roman Catholicism; in June 1973, nearly twelve thousand Roman Catholics, including some interested in the movement but not yet part of it, gathered for a charismatic conference at Notre Dame University in Indiana.

Outside the main-line Protestant groups and the Roman Catholic Church the movement has found devotees among the Jesus People and the youth groups in Europe as well as in America. It has penetrated places and institutions that have been hesitant to endorse it. Tongues-speaking appeared on evangelical college and seminary campuses and in evangelistic groups that work on campuses and in high schools. *Christianity Today's* news editor Edward Plowman has reported on its widespread existence in Europe in out of the way places as well as in cities.

Is the charismatic movement genuine? How is it to be understood in the light of Biblical revelation? How does it relate to traditional Pentecostalism? What is the significance of its rise in the Roman Catholic Church and how are Protestants to regard it in that church in the light of the Reformation and even Vatican I and II?

In the phrase "baptism in the Holy Spirit" lies the heart of the matter. Traditional Pentecostalism, represented by solid evangelical groups like the Assemblies of God (which is a long-time member of the National Association of Evangelicals), says that subsequent to the experience of salvation, of being born again,

89

there is this second experience of being baptized in the Holy Spirit. The outward evidence of this baptism is speaking in tongues. This baptism is related to sanctification, not to justification, and classic Pentecostalists say every believer should experience it.

Among the implications of this traditional Pentecostal view are these: First, not all saved people have been baptized in the Holy Spirit; those who have not are true believers but are missing something they ought to have. Second, those who have not spoken in tongues have not been baptized in the Spirit and so are defective Christians. No doubt this is what causes the great emphasis on Spirit baptism. The emphasis has not sprung from spiritual pride or a feeling of superiority, though some have slipped into these sins. Third, the traditional Pentecostal view rules out the possibility that Christians in the Keswick movement, the holiness movement, and other deeper-life movements that do not practice speaking in tongues have been Spirit-baptized. But members of these groups believe in the infilling of the Holy Spirit, believe that every Christian should be so filled, and believe there are conditions the believer must meet in order to have this experience. Many of them have had an infilling experience and are convinced that they are in no way inferior in their daily walk to those whose baptism has been accompanied by tongues-speaking.

Traditional Pentecostalism has to say that some of the greatest saints through the ages, whatever spiritual experiences they may have had, and however exalted the quality of their lives and the greatness of their ministries, were not Spirit-baptized inasmuch as they did not speak in tongues. This would include Luther, Melanchthon, Calvin, Knox, Mather, and Edwards, as well as evangelists like Wesley, Whitefield, Moody, Sunday, Chapman, Fuller, and Billy Graham.

The modern charismatic movement should be called neo-Pentecostal in that it functions outside the structures of traditional Pentecostalism, being found in most major and minor Protestant denominations, in the Roman Catholic and Orthodox churches, and outside all ecclesiastical fences as well. It is in agreement with traditional Pentecostalism on the subject of baptism in the Holy Spirit accompanied by tongues and in its emphasis on the gifts of interpretation of tongues and healing. But whether there is convergence on the basic Bible doctrines at the heart of the Christian faith is another matter that requires consideration.

We must first nail down the fact that tongues-speaking, in and out of structured Pentecostalism, can be a genuine spiritual experience, validated by Scripture, and manifested by multitudes of people whose Christian integrity and authentic life-style cannot be gainsaid. At the same time two other observations must be made. First, wherever the real exists, the counterfeit makes its appearance. There are phenomena that go by the name of the Pentecostal experience that are spurious, as the film *Marjoe* makes clear. Marjoe acknowledges that in his evangelistic campaigns he simulated tongues-speaking, and he gave a convincing demonstration in the film. But it was nothing more than a hypocritical performance. The question must be asked, How can one distinguish between the genuine and the counterfeit?

A second observation is that there are all kinds of evidence that glossolalia has never been limited to the Christian fraternity. It is found as a worldwide phenomenon among pagans, Hindu holy men, Mormons, and countless others, and some converts from the drug culture say tongues was part of their psychedelic experience.

Since it is not a uniquely Christian experience, there has to be some way the genuine can be distinguished from the counterfeit. This can be done by applying the tests of doctrine and of works to those who profess to have a gift of tongues.

William J. Samarin in his book *Tongues of Men and Angels* says that while speaking in tongues is real, the tongues spoken are not languages as known among men. Indeed, he says that the sounds the glossolalic utters lack basic elements common to all spoken languages. Tongues are ecstatic utterances, not known languages. The accounts of how people are supposed to have been given the gift of speaking in a known language are extremely hard to validate; if there have been any since Pentecost they have been few in number. And, strangely, there is no known case in which a missionary received the permanent gift of speaking the language of a group he sought to reach. Missionaries have always had to learn to speak the required languages the hard way. (Nor has any seminary student or Bible scholar ever received the gift of being able to speak and read Hebrew and Greek.)

There are all kinds of testimonies about what tongues-speaking has produced in the Christian life, and this evidence should not be treated lightly. General Ralph E. Haines, Jr., an Episcopal layman who holds one of the highest command posts in the United States Army, gave his testimony at a public meeting in Denver, having been baptized in the Holy Spirit with the accompanying sign of tongues:

> What has the baptism of the Holy Spirit done for me? I think it has made me a better man, a better husband, and more understanding of my fellow man. I am much more excited by prayer and Bible study—and I believe more perceptive in both. I am a far stronger witness for Jesus Christ. I have gained a greater joy in my Christian life. I think a Spirit-filled Christian radiates joy. Sometimes I'm so happy I think it's sinful! Then I realize there is no joy in sin. There may be fleeting pleasure, but there is no enduring joy in sin. I've learned recently that a Christian even finds joy in sorrow, in trials and tribulations.

On the other hand, the late Donald Gee of the British Assemblies of God in his book *Now That You've Been Baptized in the Spirit* (reprinted by Gospel Publishing House, 1972) candidly faces some of the problems traditional Pentecostalists have had. He acknowledges that "there is something radically wrong with the experience that gives you gifts and doesn't give you holiness." "Some Baptisms are disappointing because some people have been urged to speak in what *seemed* to be tongues, and I doubt if they have really had the Baptism at all" (p. 28, my italics). He agrees that there are Christians who have never spoken in tongues and thus have never, in his opinion, had the baptism in the Spirit, yet whose lives manifest the fruits of righteousness and the fruit of the Spirit.

> That is why people say, "Look at all those beautiful Christians with their holy lives. They have never had this Baptism." Yes, they are beautiful and we thank God for their lives. What is the explanation? They have Christ in their hearts, they are walking and living with Him. Thank God the character of Jesus Christ is revealed in our lives (p. 30).

There are, indisputably, Christians who have not spoken in

tongues whose lives in every way match up to the lives of those who *have* spoken in tongues. And there are even non-tongues-speaking Christians whose lives appear far better than the lives of some who have spoken in tongues. Why then should tongues be thought to be the necessary sign of the Holy Spirit baptism, if all that baptism signified by tongues produces has been equaled and in some cases surpassed in the lives of Christians who have never spoken in tongues?

At this point a warning flag should be raised about experience that cannot be tested by objective criteria. In reviewing *The Other Dimension: A Search for the Meaning of Religious Attitudes,* a book by Roman Catholic Louis Dupre, Clark Pinnock said the author holds that "we must not commit ourselves to biblical teachings as they stand, but must drive toward the deeper existential meaning of its mythical symbols. 'All communication from God bears the marks of ultimate incommunicability.' " One might also say something about the incommunicability of Dupre's statement. But this is characteristic of the age in which we live. Thus a popular theologian can warn us that "people who demand a higher norm of truth than human experience are asking for an idol."

Since charismatics agree that not all tongues-speaking is genuine, that there are non-tongues-speaking Christians whose lives are of the highest spiritual order, and that some who speak in tongues do not in fact show in their lives what the baptism in the Spirit is supposed to produce, we cannot let tongues be the test to determine whether one has been converted. We must get behind tongues to the Scripture and when we get to Scripture we get doctrine. And with doctrine we must now concern ourselves.

Writing about the meeting of twelve thousand Roman Catholic charismatics at Notre Dame in June 1973, Willmar Thorkelson of the *Minneapolis Star* quoted Vinson Synan, author of a very competent history entitled *The Pentecostal Holiness Movement,* as saying that he rejoiced "at the growth of Catholic Pentecostalism" and that "the Spirit of God told me it was real." But suppose someone else says it is counterfeit. Whose word shall we then take? The Old Testament abounds with evidences both of true and false prophets. Jeremiah was a true prophet, Hananiah a false one.

The test of a true prophet is whether what he prophesied comes to pass. Hananiah failed this test. The test of the tongues-speaker is not that he has spoken in tongues, for even pagans do this, but how he receives and accepts the propositional revelation of God in Holy Scripture. It is a matter of what he believes, not simply of an experience he has had.

Traditional Pentecostals hold that the baptism of the Spirit produces a change of life-style. Their beliefs have always caused them to eschew alcohol and tobacco. They are genuinely puzzled by Catholic charismatics whose Spirit baptism has not kept them from smoking cigarettes and drinking cocktails. They firmly believe that the body of the Christian is the temple of the Holy Spirit and is not to be defiled. At a time when the surgeon-general of the United States warns that tobacco is hazardous and when cigarette-induced lung cancer is at an all-time high, they do not think it amiss to ask: How can a person baptized in the Spirit so defile his body? They feel the same way about alcohol, especially in light of the alcohol addiction of millions of Americans. It is, of course, easier to focus on items like these than it is to deal with such sins as greed, selfishness, racism, gossip, and lack of love; but traditional Pentecostalism teaches that Spirit baptism makes these things inconsistent with the Christian life, too.

Surely any true baptism in the Holy Spirit will bring men to Scripture. But Protestants are convinced that parts of Catholic doctrine are un-Biblical.

Kevin Ranaghan, a Catholic charismatic lay leader, said the charismatic movement is creating "a whole new breed of evangelists and teachers" who are "permeating the church's structure in a new way." He called for the movement to remain inside the Catholic Church and wants "a weeding out" of those elements "not truly of God and not helping to build the church as a whole." He warned against the example of "eighteenth- and nineteenth-century pious Protestant groups which began to believe that the parent church was false and they had to 'come out' of it. . . . We must be one with the Catholic Church so He will be able to renew the Catholic Church, which has been His body since the day of Pentecost." To identify the Catholic Church as the Lord's

Body since Pentecost would draw strong protests from men like Luther, Calvin, Knox, and their descendants.

At the same meeting, Auxiliary Bishop Joseph C. McKinny of Grand Rapids appealed to the charismatics to "remain faithful to the leadership of the papacy." It was consonant with faithfulness to the papacy that at this meeting non-Catholics were told they would not be able to receive communion when the sacrifice of the Mass was held.

The plight of Catholic charismatics who have been regenerated and who have spoken in tongues is a painful one. Whatever the charismatic movement has to offer Roman Catholics has its origins in historic Pentecostalism, and historic Pentecostalism is at serious odds with the Roman Catholic Church in ways that cannot be glossed over. Catholic Pentecostals at last will have to bow to their church's teaching, or stay in a church some of whose teaching they cannot accept, or get out.

Hans Küng, not a charismatic but a perceptive thinker and a well-known Catholic theologian, is a case in point. He stays in the church, but he disbelieves some of what the church requires him to believe and says he cannot deny without losing his salvation. Yet Küng maintains he is the real Catholic and wants only to eliminate the false accretions that have attached themselves to church doctrine through the centuries. But there is no evidence that he or the charismatics can "weed out" those elements "not truly of God," by which we would like to think they mean, not supportable by Scripture.

Foremost among these doctrinal points that Catholic charismatics must face is that which lies at the heart of the salvatory process: justification. Catholicism teaches that men are justified because they *are* righteous. This has been known as the doctrine of infused righteousness. Reformation theology teaches *imputed* righteousness: man is not righteous in himself, indeed is unrighteous, but by his faith in Christ the righteousness of Jesus is imputed to him and he is justified. At no point in this life is the believer ever righteous in and of himself. He is declared righteous by reason of Christ's merits, for he has none of his own. He is kept by Christ's righteousness, and at last he will be glorified the same way.

The question of justification by imputed righteousness through faith cannot be side-stepped. Any speaking in tongues that is worthy of the name must be based upon a credible salvation, and there can be no salvation that is not based upon justification by faith alone. Without justification by faith alone there can be no valid tongues-speaking, Catholic, Protestant, or any other brand. For Pentecostals to accept Catholic charismatics as bona fide believers because they have spoken in tongues is to put the cart before the horse. Tongues do not prove the speaker has been justified. Acceptance in the Christian community must be based not upon tongues but upon the acceptance of imputed righteousness of Christ through faith alone.

Beyond justification by faith alone, other theological issues that Catholic charismatics must face are the sacrifice of the Mass, the infallibility of the pope, the immaculate conception, the assumption of Mary, images, and the view that tradition has a place in the church on a par with that of Scripture. Catholic charismatics must sooner or later face these teachings and decide what they believe. If they don't believe in the immaculate conception and the assumption of Mary, they lose their salvation in the eyes of the church; if they don't believe the church has the power or the right to do this, then again they put themselves outside the pale of the church. They are tied up to a comprehensive system, the denial of any vital part of which leaves them in a graceless state.

If they do accept the teaching of their church on these matters, then there is no possibility of a genuine Catholic-Protestant-Pentecostal fellowship. The reason is simple. If there were such a possibility, it would be based solely upon the baptism in the Spirit, the sign of which is speaking in tongues. This cannot be the basis for such a communion or fellowship unless the baptism in the Spirit accompanied by tongues becomes the first and the primary consideration. Since it cannot and should not be, either for Catholics or Protestants, those doctrines that precede tongues and from which tongues spring must assume their rightful role and be accorded the primacy that is due them.

In some quarters there is a tendency to make the baptism in the Spirit with tongues the sole criterion for fellowship, to make the charismatic movement ecumenical and in the process to brush

aside fundamental doctrinal questions. A well-known Pentecostalist who has devoted years of his life to promoting the charismatic movement among Protestants and Roman Catholics wrote
that in a recent Lutheran charismatic conference "the public recognized that we were all Christians by our love." Any Christian
can enthusiastically endorse the need for love. But love in the short
run can be simulated, just as tongues can be counterfeited. John
says we are known to be Christians by what we believe. "Any one
who goes ahead and does not abide in the *doctrine* of Christ does
not have God; he who abides in the *doctrine* has both the Father
and the Son. If any one comes to you and does not bring this
doctrine, do not receive him into the house or give him any greet-
ing" (II John 9-10 RSV).

This same Pentecostalist brother said: "Until now the Classic
Pentecostals found it very difficult to accept the Neo-Pentecostals
and even more difficult to accept the Catholic Pentecostals. For
ten years I have not had any official cooperation from Pentecostal
leaders." When speaking of the Pentecostal Fellowship of North
America, he expressed a glowing hope: "What a glorious day it
will be when this Fellowship opens up to all that are baptized in the
Holy Spirit from all churches and denominations. When that day
comes I shall begin to look forward to the day when the Pentecostal World Conference will be open for all that are Baptized in
the Holy Spirit. Then we shall learn to know the true unity in the
Spirit. . . ."

These assertions raise serious problems. Perhaps the writer did
not say exactly what he meant to say. First, the statement is highly
divisive because while it professes to aim toward Christian unity,
that unity is limited to those who have been baptized in the Spirit
and have spoken in tongues. This leaves out multitudes of true
believers who have not spoken in tongues, even those who believe
they have been filled with the Spirit but for whom there has been no
tongues. It excludes "Classical Pentecostalists" who believe in
tongues but have not experienced them. A fellowship that is "open
for all that are Baptized in the Holy Spirit" is, obviously, closed to
those who have not been. It comes down to this: Tongues are seen
as normative and speaking in tongues becomes the test for true
fellowship and unity. Is it not instructive that Jesus Christ might be

excluded from such a fellowship, too? He was filled with the Holy Spirit from conception and the Holy Spirit was present at His baptism, but there is no evidence that He ever spoke in a tongue.

The Assemblies of God, one of the large Pentecostal bodies, has never permitted its views on baptism in the Spirit with tongues to become a test of fellowship in its churches or outside them. This group has long been an honored member of the National Association of Evangelicals and has fruitfully labored with non-tongues-speaking groups. The Assemblies' general superintendent, Thomas F. Zimmerman, was on the central committee of the U.S. Congress on Evangelism. As late as August of 1973 the denomination issued a statement on the charismatic movement in which the emphasis was properly placed. The statement said: "It is important that we find our way in a sound scriptural path, avoiding the extremes of an ecumenism that compromises scriptural principles and an exclusivism that excludes true Christians."

What has been said about the problems that arise for Roman Catholic charismatics must also be applied to theological liberals who have spoken in tongues. This does not mean they have suddenly become theologically orthodox. For them as for anybody else the test of "the doctrine of Christ in the spirit of Christ" must be applied. No matter how many tongues a man speaks or how many times he does it, if his doctrine is defective, his tongues will not sancify his aberration. The baptism in the Spirit cannot serve as a cover for heterodox belief or sanctify the denial of Scriptural truth.

Classic Pentecostalism with few exceptions has always been evangelical in its theological position. Its adherents have taken the Bible to be the trustworthy Word of God. They have always adhered to the truths that are to be found in the historic confessions of evangelical groups through the centuries. The doctrine that has given Pentecostalism its uniqueness has been that of baptism in the Holy Spirit with tongues as the sign. Non-Pentecostal evangelicals, even those who accept the gift of tongues as the sovereign work of the Holy Spirit who bestows that or any other charismatic gift as He pleases and wills, believe that Christians are baptized by the Spirit when they are justified and regenerated, and that tongues are not a necessary sign of that baptism. They believe that Christians should be filled with the Spirit, but while tongues are not ruled out, they are not considered essential to the Spirit-filled life.

It is quite unlikely that there ever will be full agreement one way or the other about tongues and baptism in the Spirit. Those who believe in it can and should be expected not only to practice this view but also to propagate it. No evangelical need feel threatened by this emphasis because he has not spoken in tongues. If he is convinced from Scripture that he has the fullness of the Spirit without tongues, there is no reason for him to doubt it. If he is inclined toward the Pentecostal viewpoint, let him by all means seek both the baptism and tongues. But let those who have experienced tongues remember that there are Christians who have not had this experience who are filled with the joy of the Lord, experience His presence daily, and exhibit His power and love.

After the Great Awakening in New England, Jonathan Edwards wrote his classic work on religious affections. He saw the hand of Satan both in the revival and in those who fought against it; Satan sowed tares both ways to undo a true work of Christ. Edwards believed in religious affections, i.e., "experimental religion" that would surely include the Pentecostal aspect. He believed that testing the spirits is of the essence of experimental religion and so he argued, "The conduct of Christians in the world is to be guided by three demands. First, behavior must be in conformity with Christian rules; secondly, the 'practice of religion' must be the chief occupation of life; and thirdly, one must persist in this practice till the end of his earthly days" (*Jonathan Edwards: A Profile*, edited by David Levin, Hill and Wang, 1969, p. 207). If those three demands are met, both those who speak in tongues and those who do not need have no fear when they stand before the judgment seat of Jesus Christ.

9

A PROPOSAL
FOR THE TONGUES
CONTROVERSY
by Clark H. Pinnock and Grant R. Osborne

Evangelical Christians are divided against themselves. At a time when the world is hungering to hear "good news" in the midst of the secular wasteland, an acrimonious debate about the legitimacy of tongues in the Christian life divides our ranks and saps our energies. This chapter is an attempt to clear the air and raise the level of rhetoric on both sides. If the evangelical community followed the guidelines proposed, greater harmony would descend and the mission of the church would advance.

On a corporate level, it is pleasing to see signs of a growing cooperation between Pentecostals and non-Pentecostals. The involvement of Pentecostals in the National Association of Evangelicals and the leadership of Dr. Thomas Zimmerman, president of the Assemblies of God, in the international Key '73 evangelistic program are two examples of this. However, on the grass-roots level there is little cooperation and a great deal of suspicion.

Two important points must be clarified at the outset. First, the debate over whether tongues in the apostolic age and today were real languages or ecstatic utterances—which many consider crucial to the question of the validity of glossolalia today—is not really vital to the connection between the two. Actually, there is no uniformity of opinion. Frederick D. Bruner *(A Theology of the Holy Spirit,* Eerdmans, 1970) says that the charismatic movement as a whole affirms both characteristics, "even though the ecstasy may at times appear somewhat peculiar to observers and the language usually unknown to hearers." The Biblical evidence is also somewhat ambiguous. One must agree with the contention that at Ephesus Luke does not delineate the nature of the gift, nor does Paul at Corinth. Arguments may rage, but no conclusion may be drawn, for Scripture itself is silent. Today it is claimed that both types are manifest (see Morton T. Kelsey, *Tongue Speaking: An Experience in Spiritual Experience,* Doubleday, 1964, pp. 152-60, for an example of tongues as real languages). This would be possible Biblically, for while Pentecost featured known languages, I Corinthians 13:1 and 14:2 point to ecstatic speech. The important point is that the nature of the gift cannot be the criterion for veracity. This must be determined from other considerations, especially the manifestation of the fruit of the Spirit (Gal. 5:22-23) in the life of the tongue-speaker.

The other preliminary point is the supposed distinction between tongues as an initial sign of Spirit-baptism and as the gift of the Spirit. Many Pentecostals teach a definite difference, holding that according to Acts all Christians must experience the former as the necessary step to a higher Christian walk, but that the latter is given by the Spirit as a gift to the individual believer (see Article 7 of the "Statement of Faith" of the Assemblies of God). It is the thesis of this study that Scripture upholds no such distinction. The first section will show that tongues as a gift for this age is valid Biblically, whereas the second section will make the point that glossolalia as the normative, initial evidence of Spirit-baptism cannot be upheld Scripturally.

For the Non-Glossolalist

1. Tongues are a legitimate gift of the Spirit to the church today.

Those who contest the validity of the tongues movement generally do so along the lines suggested in Benjamin Warfield's *Miracles: Yesterday and Today.* He argued that miracles, including the gift of tongues, were signs designed to authenticate the apostles, and gradually ceased with the passing of that age. In addition, it is held that glossolalia, where it does appear in church history, arises in heterodox circles like the Montanists; therefore, it is concluded that the gift ceased after the canon was concluded and never truly appeared again (see Anthony Hoekema, *What About Tongue Speaking?* Eerdmans, 1966, p. 111 f.). Exegetical evidence is taken from the Book of Acts, and from I Corinthians

13:8-12, where it is asserted that Paul prophesied the imminent cessation of this gift.

These arguments are far from convincing. Not only does Paul acknowledge that tongues is a genuine spiritual gift; he also states that he himself practiced it (I Cor. 14:2, 18). His remarks against it have entirely to do with its *abuse* in the assembly. When employed in public, tongues must be accompanied with an interpretation, otherwise it is profitless for the church (v. 27).

Moreover, the New Testament nowhere teaches that the gifts were given solely to authenticate the apostles or that they were to cease after the apostolic age. Geoffrey W. Bromiley writes,

> Scripture does not explicitly restrict these gifts to the apostles or their day, and hence we have no ground on which to limit the sovereign disposing of the Spirit. . . . Though we may not command or claim the charismata, or any specific charisma, the Spirit's donation may still be looked for as and when he himself decides (*The Fundamentals of the Faith,* ed. by Carl F. H. Henry, Zondervan, 1969, p. 159).

Irenaeus, in his *Against Heresies,* mentions "many brethren in the Church . . . who through the Spirit speak all kinds of languages." John Calvin in his commentary on I Corinthians not only regarded glossolalia as a legitimate gift of the Spirit but wrote against those who "declaim against them with furious zeal," saying: "Paul, nevertheless, commands the use of tongues. So far is he from wishing them abolished or thrown away." In his journal for November 25, 1795, John Wesley noted the occurrence of tongues and expressed the opinion that the danger was less an over-emphasis than a suppression or denial of spiritual gifts.

Finally, Paul does not teach the cessation of tongues in particular at the close of the apostolic age. First Corinthians 13 is a bridge passage between his remarks on the distribution of gifts (chap. 12) and their regulation (chap. 14). In it the apostle indicates that love is the context in which all the gifts must be exercised. The only cessation to which he refers is that which occurs at the coming of Christ (v. 10).

Our approach to tongues must be an open-minded, inductive exegesis of the Biblical text. Outright repudiation is un-Scriptural.

2. The glossolalist should be welcomed into Christian fellowship and accepted into all cooperative endeavors.

Divisions over the tongues question are due as much to the harsh condemnation meted out by non-glossolalists as to anything else. Tongues is not a matter of fundamental truth and thus cannot be determinative of fellowship. Contrary to popular opinion, most glossolalists do not weave their entire theology or personal religion around this gift. An even superficial acquaintance with the movement will make clear the centrality of Christ. Honesty requires us to admit that very often there is an exuberance and joy in charismatic circles for which all believers deeply yearn. Instead of condemning and ostracizing, let us put glossolalists to the test: welcome them into worship, fellowship, and service. That is the only Christian way.

There is a caricature that must be smashed. Many Christians look down on the glossolalist as a neurotic, insecure person who can express himself only in unseemly emotional ways. But some psychological tests have indicated that the opposite may be true. Glossolalists do not suffer from a higher incidence of abnormal personality than other people, and in many cases the gift as a religious experience seems to contribute to mental health (see L. M. Vav Eetveldt Vivier, *Glossolalia,* unpublished doctoral dissertation, University of Chicago, 1960, and E. Mansell Pattison, "Behavioral Scientific Research on the Nature of Glossolalia," *Journal of the American Scientific Affiliation,* XX, 1968, 73-86). Hyperemotionalism is no necessary ingredient of tongues.

There is a tendency also to practice social discrimination with glossolalists. They are thought to belong only to the lower strata of society, economically and intellectually. The prominence of leaders such as Dennis Bennett, Episcopal rector from Seattle, and the appearance of the gift on prestigious campuses throughout the United States reveal this as a baseless charge.

Speaking practically, of course, there are distinctives that make difficult a united worship of Pentecostals and non-Pentecostals. Differing styles of church meeting have developed along denominational lines, just as have differences over the sacraments. However, this need have no bearing on interdenominational fellowship and cooperation; there is a very real basis for unity in all major issues. Moreover, churches need not split when tongues break out within them. Paul left room within the worship service for such manifestations (I Cor. 14:26, 39), so long as certain guidelines were followed—edification (14:5, 26), interpretation (14:5, 13, 28), self-control (14:27), order (14:40), and the absence of proselytizing (12:18-31). This last is the foundation stone of combined worship and continued unity. Anyone who insists on propagating his distinctive practice—be it tongues, a certain mode of baptism, or foot-washing—removes himself from those who do not practice such. The proper view of glossolalia will recognize it as an individual gift depending on the sovereign choice of the Spirit, not a corporate experience every Christian must undergo.

On the positive side, it is impossible to ignore the place of tongues in several highly significant evangelistic movements of our day. The young Jesus People, a large body of newly converted Christians, belong, for the most part, to the charismatic movement. It is difficult, after reading David Wilkerson's *The Cross and the Switchblade,* to doubt that tongues has played a role in the rehabilitation of many drug addicts.

At the end of Paul's discussion of the problem, he commands that tongues not be forbidden (I Cor. 14:39). Granted, it is not the best gift with which to edify the church. Nevertheless, it has validity and should be gratefully received by all Christians as coming from God.

For the Glossolalist

1. Tongues-speaking is not the normative sign of Spirit baptism.

Here we must consider the first aspect of the Pentecostal distinction, that the universal, initial sign of Spirit baptism, itself subsequent to salvation, is tongues. As such it differs from the gift of the experience, given only to some. In all fairness, however, it must be said that many Pentecostals insist that the experience should continue to be enjoyed after the initial reception. Bruner (p. 144) writes, "This reasoning is not difficult to follow, for given the necessity of the evidence of tongues in the Spirit baptism, not to continue speaking in tongues after having begun seems to be not only unspiritual but unnatural, indicating, it is sometimes argued, a lack of faith (Mark 16:17) and of obedience (I Cor. 14:5)."

The Book of Acts is held to demonstrate the normative value of tongues. Six special passages are used to defend its necessity —Acts 2 (Pentecost), 4:31 (the second Pentecost), 8 (Samaria), 9 (conversion of Saul), 10—11 (conversion of Cornelius), and 19 (the "Ephesian Pentecost"). Pentecostals argue that in every case in Acts, tongues were present as the conspicuous evidence of the power of the Spirit's coming upon the individual. Also, they teach that this is meant for every age of the church.

This argument is weak methodologically and exegetically. Didactic portions of Scripture must have precedence over historical passages in establishing doctrine. We ought to move here from the teaching of I Corinthians to the narrative of Acts rather than the reverse. When one follows this proper methodology, one notes that there is no manifestation of tongues that is normative. Each member of the Body of Christ, according to Paul, enjoys a manifestation of the Spirit for the common good (I Cor. 12:7, 11). There is not one gift that all Christians share (v. 19 f.) Glossolalia is simply *not* normative. The infallible sign of spiritual fullness is moral and religious (see Gal. 5:22—6:2; Eph. 5:18-20; Col. 3:16). It is germane to point out that the Corinthian Christians, with their overemphasis, tended to be carnal and unspiritual (I Cor. 3:1-4).

More important to the issue, the Book of Acts does not establish a normative experience for the believer today. Without doubt Acts describes the appearance of glossolalia on at least three important occasions (2:4-13; 10:46; 19:6). It is only fair to point out, however, that in the other instances alluded to by Pentecostals, Scripture does not mention tongues and does not require such a manifestation. Moreover, each of the three cases mentioned above was a special circumstance that marked a turning point in the spread of the gospel. The appearance of glossolalia in each instance meant God's authentication of that progression of the gospel.

Three further points may be gleaned from the evidence of Acts. For one thing, there is a significant absence of the "seeking" of tongues, a central Pentecostal distinctive. There is no record that any person sought the gift, according to the primary passages —Acts 2, 8, 10, and 19. Also, there is no evidence of a Spirit baptism subsequent to salvation. The phenomenon in many instances accompanies salvation, as in the case of Cornelius and

Paul. Moreover, there may be repeated fillings (e.g., Acts 4:31) that are not equated with charismatic gifts. Finally, it is striking how often the outpouring of the Spirit is referred to where glossolalia is not mentioned (see, for example, Acts 2:41; 4:4; 6:7; 8:36; 9:42).

We may conclude that the historical narrative of Acts does not establish the normative role of tongues. Indeed, Acts seems to stress bold witness as a sign of spiritual depth (4:31). This explains the success in the lives of men like Wesley, Moody, Torrey, Graham—each of whom has known the fullness of the Spirit and yet has not been reported to have spoken in other tongues. Men such as these are living proof that this exegesis is correct—there is no Spirit baptism subsequent to salvation that is initially evidenced by tongues.

2. The glossolalist should not take a superior attitude toward those who have not experienced tongues, nor should he coerce others to do so.

It must be stated that Pentecostals themselves are among the harshest critics of such a "spiritual aristocracy" attitude among adherents. One can easily understand how the person who accepts tongues as the only initial evidence of Spirit baptism and as a natural subsequent experience could come to look on the person who hasn't experienced it as spiritually stunted.

However, it is the thesis of this study that glossolalia is not to be sought nor propagated. Of course, one must expect Pentecostals, given their doctrinal stand, to propagate their views; they could hardly do otherwise. The purpose here is to seek the Biblical standard against which these views must be examined.

The Book of Acts shows, as we have already seen, that tongues was never sought in the apostolic age. First Corinthians 12—14 places the historical description there on a doctrinal plane. A brief perusal of this passage will establish Paul's view of tongues. In chapter 12 he discusses the distribution of the gifts of the Spirit, focusing on tongues. In 12:4-11 he teaches that this, like all other gifts, is given according to the sovereign choice of the Spirit rather than the individual desire of man. Verses 12-27 add that each person has a separate function, and that the various gifts distributed to different men unite in a combined whole; the gifts are separately given but corporately united, each with its part in the Body of Christ. The conclusion is seen in verses 28-31, which definitely show that no gift is meant to be universally distributed. In verse 30, which should be translated "All do not speak in tongues, do they?" the principle is enunciated that this gift is meant only particularly and not universally.

Chapter 13, usually separated from its context, is meant to establish the principle that must guide the exercise of these gifts: self-giving love. In verses 1-3 tongues is placed among other gifts and is not seen as universal any more than the others. The last part of the chapter, beginning with verse 8, then continues this theme, pointing to tongues as one among many gifts, all of which cease at the Parousia, when they will be absorbed by love.

Finally, chapter 14 applies this practically. While an exegesis of this comprehensive passage is not possible here, a few significant points may be made. First, glossolalia must not be practiced publicly apart from interpretation, and its goal must always be edification (v. 1-13). Furthermore, it is better for private use than for public demonstration (v. 14-19), because in public it is a negative sign that will only further the unbeliever in his state (v. 20-25). Finally, the very strict regulations governing its public manifestation are relevant to this study—the restriction of the number who may speak, the necessity of an interpreter and of rational judgment regarding the proceedings, the prohibition against speaking (a point whose applicability to our time is controversial), women, and the overriding importance of order in the service (v. 26-40).

These chapters presuppose the limited distribution and use of this particular gift. There is no room for active seeking, only for passive waiting for the particular gift the sovereign Spirit bestows on each one. This is intended for both the initial baptism, which is not sought but is automatically received at conversion, and for the gift, which is different for each individual. In view of such considerations, it is common sense to insist that the value of this gift be soberly measured and its practice carefully controlled. "The spirits of the prophets are subject to the prophets" (14:32).

Conclusion

Non-glossolalists run the risk of quenching the Spirit (I Thess.

5:19-21). So long as the Biblical safeguards are observed, there is no reason why glossolalia should alarm us or hinder the work of God. Glossolalists for their part often place too great an emphasis on the gift and engage in un-Scriptural proselytizing. It is clear that the spirit of I Corinthians 13 is to condition and control this discussion between brethren. A. B. Simpson was right when he wrote:

> We believe the Scripture teaching to be that the gift of tongues is one of the gifts of the Spirit, and that it may be present in the normal Christian assembly as a sovereign bestowal of the Holy Spirit upon such as he wills. We do not believe that there is any Scriptural evidence for the teaching that speaking in tongues is the sign of having been filled with the Spirit, nor do we believe that it is the plan of God that all Christians should possess the gift of tongues. This gift is one of many gifts and is given to some for the benefit of all. The attitude toward the gift of tongues held by pastor and people should be, "Seek not, forbid not" (quoted in the *Alliance Witness,* May 1, 1963, p. 19).

BIBLIOGRAPHY

Tongues: Updating Some Old Issues .... *Eternity* editorial

The New Charismatics .... James W. L. Hills

> Reprinted by permission from *Eternity* Magazine, Copyright 1973, The Evangelical Foundation, 1716 Spruce Street, Philadelphia, PA 19103.

> The Rev. James W. L. Hills is pastor of Bethlehem Presbyterian Church, Buffalo, NY.

Facing the Issue of Tongues .... Stanley Gundry

> Reprinted from *Moody Monthly,* Copyright 1973 by Moody Bible Institute. Used by permission.

> Stanley Gundry is a faculty member of the Moody Bible Institute.

The Use and Abuse of Tongues ...... Theodore Epp and John I. Paton

> Reprinted by permission of Back to the Bible Broadcast.

> Dr. Theodore Epp is the founder and director of the Back to the Bible Broadcast.

Tongues-Speaking .... Richard W. De Haan

> Reprinted by permission of the Radio Bible Class.

> Richard W. De Haan is president and teacher of the Radio Bible Class.

Is the Charismatic Movement of God? .... Dick Meier

> Reprinted by permission from *Christian Life* Magazine, Copyright September 1973, and abridged from article, "Is the Charismatic Movement of God? No, Says This Baptist Minister; Yes, Says This Lutheran Professor," Gundersen Drive and Schmale Road, Wheaton, IL 60187.

> Dr. Dick Meier is pastor of the Open Door Baptist Church, Kansas City, Kansas.

Tests for the Tongues Movement .... Harold Lindsell

> Copyright 1972 by *Christianity Today;* reprinted by permission.

> Dr. Harold Lindsell is the editor-publisher of *Christianity Today*.

A Proposal for the Tongues Controversy .... Clark Pinnock
.... and Grant R. Osborne

> Copyright 1971 by *Christianity Today;* reprinted by permission.

> Dr. Clark Pinnock is professor of Systematic Theology at Trinity Evangelical Divinity School. Grant R. Osborne is an instructor in Greek at Trinity.